Personality Disorders

Lydia Bjornlund

Diseases and Disorders

ReferencePoint
Press

© 2011 ReferencePoint Press, Inc.
Printed in the United States

For more information, contact:
ReferencePoint Press, Inc.
PO Box 27779
San Diego, CA 92198
www.ReferencePointPress.com

Picture credits:
Cover: Dreamstime and iStockphoto.com
Maury Aaseng: 32–33, 34–35, 47–48, 61–62, 77–79
© Corbis/Laurence Mouton: 18
© Corbis/Pictorium: 11

LIBRARY OF CONGRESS CATALOGING-IN-PUBLICATION DATA

Bjornlund, Lydia D.
    Personality disorders / by Lydia Bjornlund.
        p. cm. — (Compact research series)
    Includes bibliographical references and index.
    ISBN-13: 978-1-60152-139-2 (hardcover)
    ISBN-10: 1-60152-139-1 (hardcover)
    1. Personality disorders—Juvenile literature. I. Title.
    RC554.B56   2011
    616.85'82—dc22

                                                         2010031384

Contents

Foreword

❝Where is the knowledge we have lost in information?❞

—T.S. Eliot, "The Rock."

As modern civilization continues to evolve, its ability to create, store, distribute, and access information expands exponentially. The explosion of information from all media continues to increase at a phenomenal rate. By 2020 some experts predict the worldwide information base will double every 73 days. While access to diverse sources of information and perspectives is paramount to any democratic society, information alone cannot help people gain knowledge and understanding. Information must be organized and presented clearly and succinctly in order to be understood. The challenge in the digital age becomes not the creation of information, but how best to sort, organize, enhance, and present information.

ReferencePoint Press developed the *Compact Research* series with this challenge of the information age in mind. More than any other subject area today, researching current issues can yield vast, diverse, and unqualified information that can be intimidating and overwhelming for even the most advanced and motivated researcher. The *Compact Research* series offers a compact, relevant, intelligent, and conveniently organized collection of information covering a variety of current topics ranging from illegal immigration and deforestation to diseases such as anorexia and meningitis.

The series focuses on three types of information: objective single-author narratives, opinion-based primary source quotations, and facts and statistics. The clearly written objective narratives provide context and reliable background information. Primary source quotes are carefully selected and cited, exposing the reader to differing points of view. And facts and statistics sections aid the reader in evaluating perspectives. Presenting these key types of information creates a richer, more balanced learning experience.

For better understanding and convenience, the series enhances information by organizing it into narrower topics and adding design features that make it easy for a reader to identify desired content. For example, in *Compact Research: Illegal Immigration*, a chapter covering the economic impact of illegal immigration has an objective narrative explaining the various ways the economy is impacted, a balanced section of numerous primary source quotes on the topic, followed by facts and full-color illustrations to encourage evaluation of contrasting perspectives.

The ancient Roman philosopher Lucius Annaeus Seneca wrote, "It is quality rather than quantity that matters." More than just a collection of content, the *Compact Research* series is simply committed to creating, finding, organizing, and presenting the most relevant and appropriate amount of information on a current topic in a user-friendly style that invites, intrigues, and fosters understanding.

Personality Disorders at a Glance

Recognizing Personality Disorders

Personality disorders are characterized by behaviors that are odd or eccentric, dramatic or erratic, or fearful and anxious.

Prevalence

Estimates vary widely, but most experts believe that from 9 to 15 percent of American adults suffer from at least one personality disorder.

Types of Personality Disorders

The manual used by U.S. psychiatrists recognizes 10 personality disorders: paranoid, schizoid, schizotypal, antisocial, borderline, histrionic, narcissistic, avoidant, dependent, and obsessive-compulsive personality disorder.

Most Common Personality Disorders

Borderline personality disorder and avoidant personality disorder appear to be the most common disorders, affecting more than 1 in 20 Americans.

Causes

There is no one cause of personality disorders. They appear to have both a genetic and environmental basis.

Severity

Personality disorders vary greatly in terms of severity. Borderline personality disorder is often considered the most serious because of the high risk of suicide and reckless behavior.

Onset

The onset of personality disorders is usually late adolescence or young adulthood, although many people begin to exhibit the patterns of thoughts and behaviors of the disorder in childhood.

Health Risks

People with personality disorders are at greater risk of depression, anxiety, and other mood disorders; substance abuse and addiction; and eating disorders. They also are at greater risk of obesity, heart disease, and other physical ailments.

Treatment

Psychotherapy is the cornerstone of most treatment approaches for personality disorder, although drugs may be used to alleviate some of the symptoms.

Overview

Like many people with personality disorders, Amanda Wang always felt different from others. She felt empty inside, insignificant, and confused about who she was. "I felt like something was wrong with me," she says. "It would start out with something small, and it would kind of escalate and I would be thinking that I was the worst person in the world, and that I wasn't good enough. . . . I didn't think that I had a mental disorder. . . . I just knew that I didn't like being in the body I was in."[1]

At the age of 27, after being hospitalized and deep in a crisis, Wang was diagnosed with borderline personality disorder. With treatment, Wang has been able to wrestle with her thoughts of suicide and her raw emotions, but she writes that it is a daily struggle. On her blog, which she began to help educate others about the illness and inspire those suffering from it to make positive changes, Wang writes of the struggle to cope with the intense emotions she feels:

> I've got a confession to make. There are times, many times, that I can positively say how much I hate myself. I feel like I don't deserve to be alive. I feel like if I left today, no one would notice. I don't really matter. I'm not worth it. . . . It's a difficult thing to do, to go against your urges. It's as if the whole world was conspiring against you, rooting for you to give in to them.[2]

What Are Personality Disorders?

Everyone has patterns in attitudes, emotions, thoughts, and behaviors—collectively, these make up a person's personality. People with a personality disorder interpret and respond to people and situations in substantially different ways from the majority of the population. Their attitudes and behavior may be odd or eccentric, dramatic or erratic, anxious or inhibited, and often socially unacceptable.

The American Psychiatric Association (APA) defines a personality disorder as "an enduring pattern of inner experience and behavior that deviates markedly from the expectation of the individual's culture, is pervasive and inflexible, has an onset in adolescence or early adulthood, is stable over time, and leads to distress or impairment."[3] The APA identifies 10 personality disorders: antisocial, avoidant, borderline, dependent, histrionic, narcissistic, obsessive-compulsive, paranoid, schizoid, and schizotypal. The symptoms of these disorders vary widely, but each is characterized by entrenched patterns of thinking and behavior that interfere with a person's ability to function.

Understanding of Personality Disorders Develops

Descriptions of individuals with various forms of personality disorder have been found in medical journals in most cultures and date as far back as ancient Greece. Early psychologists believed that personality disorders were a mild form of psychoses, such as schizophrenia, and neuroses, such as anxiety and depressive disorders. The first modern analysis came about in 1938, when American psychoanalyst Adolph Stern described the symptoms of patients that he believed to be on the border between neurosis and psychosis—the two categories of mental illness at the time. He described such patients as "extremely difficult to handle effectively by any psychotherapeutic method."[4] Although mental health professionals no longer believe in this assessment, the name "borderline" began to be used for one form of personality disorder.

> " People with a personality disorder interpret and respond to people and situations in substantially different ways from the majority of the population. "

Over the next several decades, mental health experts built on Stern's understanding to specify the characteristics and impairments that define personality disorders. In the 1970s psychiatrists identified mechanisms to diagnose personality disorders. Diagnostic criteria for personality disorders were first included in the 1980 edition of the *Diagnostic and Statistical Manual (DSM)*, which is the standard classification of mental disorders used by mental health professionals in the United States. The most recent edition divides mental illnesses into various axes, or categories. Personality disorders are categorized as Axis II disorders. The World Health Organization provides similar classification, and similar diagnostic criteria, for the international community.

Characteristics and Symptoms

Some people with personality disorders—even severe cases—function well in some settings. People with mild forms of a personality disorder may have successful careers and families, but the more severe the symptoms are, the more difficult it is to cope. In fact, one of the diagnostic criteria for a personality disorder is that the disorder interferes with a person's ability to function.

The fact that people with a personality disorder perceive the world differently from others can make it difficult for a person with a disorder to sustain close, meaningful relationships. Sometimes, it is only a loving parent or spouse who sees the most severe symptoms of uncontrolled anger or rage. The symptoms of a personality disorder also often undermine success in the workplace. Not surprisingly, personality disorders are associated with failures to reach potential.

Personality disorders are characterized by self-destructive and self-denigrating patterns of thought and behavior. These patterns interfere with routine functioning at work, at school, and in social situations.

The characteristics for the various personality disorders vary considerably, but they all have several features in common. Self-centeredness—me-first behaviors and self-absorption—is a cornerstone of most personality disorders. People with a personality disorder tend to lack empathy for others and accountability for their actions. This often results in behavior that others see as manipulative or exploitative. People with personality disorders have a distorted understanding of themselves and others. Even when the symptoms are mild, people with personality disorders typically feel a general sense of unhappiness, often manifested as depression or an anxiety disorder.

Many of the symptoms evident in an adult with a personality disorder are consistent from birth. In interviews parents of disordered adults often tell researchers that their adult child has had the same extreme behaviors, temperament, and problems since birth.

In addition to anecdotal evidence from interviews with parents and family members, researchers have attempted to observe behaviors themselves to see whether they can predict a causal relationship between unusual behaviors in children and a diagnosis as adults. One study that began in the 1980s observed subjects as toddlers and then, 25 years later, as adults. The study showed that the elements common to antisocial personality disorder were evident in the temperament of children as young as three years of age. A disproportionate number of these children went on to develop conduct disorder as teens.

Comparison with Other Mental Illnesses

Recent research has strengthened the understanding of personality disorders and their symptoms, but they remain difficult to diagnose and treat. Indeed, some clinicians continue to argue that personality disorders do not exist—that the label is given to describe difficult patients with symptoms that are more severe than and/or atypical of mental illness. Others believe that personality disorders are better described as extreme manifestations of personality traits shared by all people than as a form of mental illness. The mainstream mental health profession has accepted personality disorders as real psychological disturbances with biological roots, however.

Some experts speculate that personality disorders may be mild forms of Axis I disorders, which include depression, anxiety disorders, bipolar disorder, attention-deficit/hyperactivity disorder (ADHD), autism spectrum disorders, phobias, and schizophrenia. There are some fundamental differences, however. Whereas the thought processes of a schizophrenic are totally out of touch with reality, those with personality disorders do not suffer from hallucinations or delusions.

> " **Personality disorders are among the most frequent disorders treated by psychiatrists.** "

The fears of a disordered personality tend to be grounded in reality. For example, a person with paranoid personality disorder might be suspicious of others' motives, but the disordered person stops short of a paranoid schizophrenic's belief that there is some kind of elaborate plot against him or her. Similarly, persons with a narcissistic personality disorder might exaggerate their self-worth, but they do not think they are someone else entirely.

People also often confuse obsessive-compulsive personality disorder and obsessive-compulsive disorder (OCD). The two share many symptoms and characteristics, but the obsessions and compulsions that are at the heart of OCD are not present in obsessive-compulsive personality disorder. As with other forms of personality disorders, people with ob-

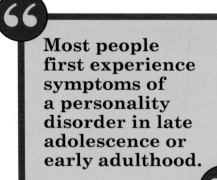

Most people first experience symptoms of a personality disorder in late adolescence or early adulthood.

sessive-compulsive personality disorder are unaware that their thinking is abnormal and insist that their way of doing things is the right way; those with OCD do not assume that their way is right.

How Common Are Personality Disorders?

The prevalence of personality disorders was largely unknown until recently, and estimates vary considerably. In general, experts estimate that 9 to 15 percent of American adults suffer from at least one personality disorder, although some experts say that current estimates of personality disorders may be too low.

As a group, personality disorders are among the most frequent disorders treated by psychiatrists. Borderline personality disorder (BPD) appears to be the most prevalent disorder in treatment settings: an estimated 20 percent of people hospitalized for mental illness suffer from BPD.

Many people suffer from several personality disorders at the same time. They also often have other mental health problems, including depression and other mood disorders, substance abuse, and eating disorders. Studies suggest that many patients who receive treatment for other causes may have an undiagnosed personality disorder.

What Are the Causes of Personality Disorders?

Personality disorders have always existed, but their causes have never been fully understood. Most experts today believe that personality disorders are caused by a combination of physical and environmental factors.

Some disorders tend to run in families, suggesting that genetics may play an important role. The environment also influences the development of a personality disorder. A disorder may be triggered by stressful life events, drug abuse, or physical illness. Experts believe that one's experiences as a child may be particularly influential. Studies have shown that a higher percentage of people with personality disorders than the average population suffered child abuse or neglect. Of course, not everyone who is abused as a child will develop a personality disorder. Nor does a stable, healthy childhood free of abuse mean that a person has no risk of being diagnosed with a disorder. It appears that if the biological risk of developing a personality disorder is very high, environmental factors may play little if any role.

> **One of the defining characteristics of a personality disorder is that it disrupts one's ability to function.**

Genetic and environmental factors likely play a role in all personality disorders, but they appear to have varying effects. According to Theodore Millon, a researcher and editor of the book *Personality-Guided Psychology*, genetic factors may increase vulnerability to some disorders, such as anti-social personality disorder, whereas others, such as dependent personality disorder, appear to be more environmentally influenced.

At-Risk Populations

Although personality disorders impact a broad spectrum of society, experts have identified some factors that may put a person at higher risk than others. Like other forms of mental illness, personality disorders appear to be inherited. This means that a person with a parent who has a disorder may be more likely to develop the disorder. In addition, there is evidence that victims of child abuse or neglect have a higher risk of developing a disorder.

Most people first experience symptoms of a personality disorder in late adolescence or early adulthood. Personality disorders often are not diagnosed until several years later, when symptoms become more severe and undermine one's ability to function. With or without diagnosis, many people with some mild forms of personality disorders are better able to function when they reach middle age.

Personality disorders affect both men and women, but some forms appear to be more prevalent in one gender than another. Paranoid, narcissistic, and antisocial personality disorders are diagnosed more often in men than women—in fact, three times as many men as women are diagnosed with antisocial personality disorder. On the other hand, more women than men are diagnosed with BPD and histrionic personality disorder. Experts believe that the differences may be largely influenced by one's social environment, but research is also looking at differences in brain function as a factor in these discrepancies.

What Are the Effects of Personality Disorders?

The number and severity of symptoms of any given personality disorder vary considerably from one individual to another. Diagnosis for dependent personality disorder, for instance, requires a patient to have just five of eight listed criteria. The diagnostic criteria for this personality disorder in the *Diagnostic and Statistical Manual of Mental Disorders (DSM)* include items such as "has difficulty making everyday decisions without an excessive amount of advice and reassurance from others, . . .

needs others to assume responsibility for most major areas of his or her life . . . [and] has difficulty expressing disagreement with others because of fear of loss of support or approval."[5] A patient with mild symptoms in the minimum number of criteria is much more likely to be able to function than someone who has severe symptoms in all eight areas.

In some cases symptoms may not be ever-present; rather, they may occur episodically in a person who otherwise exhibits relatively normal behavior.

> " Most people only seek help after the disorder has caused a major disruption in their lives—perhaps after losing a job or important relationship. "

Often these episodes result from a stressful or traumatic event—real or perceived. Experts warn that if left untreated, however, symptoms typically increase in number and severity.

One of the defining characteristics of a personality disorder is that it disrupts one's ability to function. Interpersonal conflicts and mental breakdowns may undermine a person's ability to hold down a job and make marriage and other relationships difficult. Often, people with un-diagnosed and untreated personality disorders find themselves on the fringe of society. Studies have revealed a higher-than-average prevalence of personality disorders among the poor and homeless populations.

People with personality disorders also are at higher risk of mental and physical health issues. Anxiety, depression, and mood disorders are com-mon, as is substance abuse. The high-risk behavior associated with some disorders often exacerbates existing problems and contributes to further health problems.

Family and Friends

Personality disorders can be as stressful for family and friends as for the person suffering from the disorder. The mood swings of a person with histrionic or borderline personality disorder can make it difficult for oth-ers to know what to expect. People with some BPD can become verbally or even physically abusive.

The symptoms of a personality disorder often result in the alienation of friends and further isolate the person with the disorder. One father writes of the impact of his son's disorder: "His friends come and go because he can be overbear-ing, obnoxious, manipulative, and opinionated. So he depends on us for money and emotional support. We're all he has left."[6]

Family members are often the first—and perhaps only—people to recognize the distorted thinking and behavior patterns of a person with a personality disorder. Par-ents, spouses, and siblings often play a critical role in getting a per-son into therapy and supporting him or her through the difficult

> "It can take years of intensive psy-chotherapy for a person suffering from a personality disorder to re-place established patterns of think-ing and behaving with new, more ef-fective strategies."

process of breaking down old patterns and learning new ones. While family support and involvement may be helpful in treating any mental illness, experts emphasize that it may be particularly critical for people with a personality disorder. Family members may have to learn new patterns of relating to the patient. They are also often instrumental in giving the therapist important information about a patient's history and relationship patterns.

Can People Overcome Personality Disorders?

Until about 10 or 20 years ago, most mental health professionals believed that personality disorders could not be treated. Because paranoia, suspicion, and distrust are hallmarks of many personality disorders, patients can be particularly difficult to reach with conventional therapies, but recent studies show that people can and do recover with appropriate treatment. Because different types of personality disorders benefit from different approaches, effective treatment depends on accurate diagnosis of the disorder as well as whether other conditions such as depression, anxiety, or substance abuse exist.

For any type of personality disorder, treatment is generally more effective before behaviors are entrenched and symptoms are severe. It is rare for people with personality disorders to seek treatment at the onset of the disorder, however. Most people only seek help after the disorder has caused a major disruption in their lives—perhaps after losing a job or important relationship. Others may seek help to deal with substance abuse or other problems. Still others may be forced into treatment after an antisocial act or suicide attempt.

There is currently no standard treatment for personality disorder, but patients with some types of these disorders have improved through psychotherapy, including transference-based psychotherapy, cognitive behavioral therapy, and dialectical based therapy. Antidepressants, mood stabilizers, and antipsychotic drugs are sometimes used to help reduce symptoms, but most experts advise that drugs alone are usually ineffective in treating a personality disorder.

The Road to Recovery

Mental health experts caution that recovery is usually a long process. It can take years of intensive psychotherapy for a person suffering from a

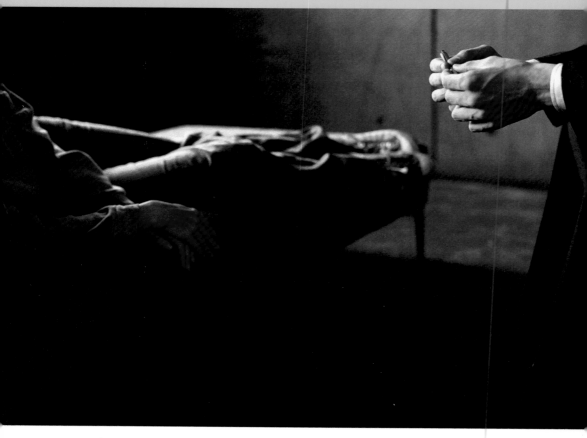

With appropriate treatment, people can and do recover from personality disorders. Psychotherapy is a major component of most treatments for personality disorders, although drugs may be used to alleviate some symptoms.

personality disorder to replace established patterns of thinking and behaving with new, more effective strategies. A.J. Mahari, who was diagnosed with BPD at age 19, describes her own path to recovery:

> I was in and out of therapy from the age of 17. It wasn't until I hit . . . bottom at the age of 33 that I opened up to the serious process of really doing the work in therapy [and] I got on the road to . . . what would be total recovery by the age of 38. . . . The next two years, from age 38 to 40 were years in which I was still solidifying the gains of recovery and further growing into the authentic me I had become.[7]

As with any mental or physical illness, a host of factors influence the prognosis for recovery. In general, people with severe symptoms will have a longer and more difficult road to recovery. A personality disorder can be more difficult to treat when the patient has a long history of unsuccessful relationships. Patients who have had consistent symptoms since childhood also may not have a pattern of successful behavior on which to build. Prognosis also tends to be poorer among patients with a family history of mental illness.

While therapists once offered little hope for people with severe forms of personality disorder, new studies show that, given the right treatment and support, people can recover. Recovery may take years of hard work on the part of the patient and his or her family, but those who have made the journey say the benefits are well worth the effort.

What Are Personality Disorders?

❝Those who struggle with a personality disorder have great difficulty dealing with other people. They tend to be inflexible, rigid, and unable to respond to the changes and demands of life. Although they feel that their behavior patterns are 'normal' or 'right,' people with personality disorders tend to have a narrow view of the world and find it difficult to participate in social activities.❞

—Mental Health America, a nonprofit organization dedicated to helping people live mentally healthier lives.

❝Personality disorders are real mental disorders, and can be both debilitating and dangerous to self and others.❞

—Stephen Diamond, *a clinical and forensic psychologist in Los Angeles.*

People with personality disorders have long-lasting and rigid patterns of thinking, feeling, and behaving that undermine their ability to function. A diagnosis is usually made when thoughts and behaviors lead to negative consequences. The erratic and/or fearful thoughts of people with personality disorders make it difficult for them to relate to other people. Many symptoms also undermine the ability to function in a work or social setting. The symptoms can be relatively mild, affecting just one area of a person's life, or so severe that the individual cannot function in any aspect of his or her life.

Personality disorders are different from psychotic disorders, which are generally considered to be a more serious and persistent form of mental illness. The delusions and hallucinations common to psychotic disorders are not present in personality disorders.

The *DSM* identifies 10 distinct personality disorders, grouped into three categories, or clusters. The clusters are based on common behaviors seen in people with personality disorders. Cluster A includes odd or eccentric behaviors. Cluster B includes dramatic or erratic behaviors. Cluster C includes fearful or anxious behaviors.

Cluster A: Odd or Eccentric Behaviors

Disorders in Cluster A are characterized by odd and eccentric behaviors. The disorders in this cluster are paranoid personality disorder, which is characterized by a pattern of suspiciousness of others' motives; schizoid personality disorder, characterized by a pattern of detachment from social relationships and normal emotions; and schizotypal personality disorder, characterized by a pattern of acute discomfort in close relationships combined with distorted perceptions and reasoning and eccentric behavior.

Some psychologists believe that Ted Kaczynski, known to the world as the Unabomber, offers an extreme example of schizoid or schizotypal personality disorder. Kaczynski shunned society. He lived deep in the woods in a shack without running water or electricity. Even prior to moving into the woods, Kaczynski had never seemed to fit in with society. "He had always been described as 'aloof,' even as a child, felt emotionally

> **Like antisocial personalities, people with BPD seem to have little control over their impulses, but their anger is more likely to be focused inward.**

abused by his parents, and was cruelly teased by his peers for being different,"[8] writes forensic psychologist Stephen Diamond. Kaczynski had sought treatment for depression and other problems, but his personality disorder went undiagnosed.

Kaczynski's thoughts and behaviors went against societal norms. He firmly believed that technology was going to cause the downfall of humanity. His eccentric thoughts led him to set about protecting the world by sending homemade pipe bombs to academic and business leaders in computer and technology fields. For almost two decades, Kaczynski waged war on technology leaders, until he was caught in 1996.

Cluster B: Dramatic or Erratic Behaviors

Cluster B disorders are characterized by dramatic, emotional, or erratic behaviors. This cluster includes antisocial personality disorder, characterized by a disregard for society's norms and other people; borderline personality disorder (BPD), characterized by pervasive instability in moods and emotions, a lack of strong identity, and chronic impulsive behavior; histrionic personality disorder, characterized by extreme emotions and attention-seeking behaviors; and narcissistic personality disorder, characterized by a pattern of grandiosity, egocentric behavior, and the need for admiration.

Psychologists for many years have struggled to understand the behaviors typical of Cluster B personalities. Much of the research devoted to personality disorders has focused on the antisocial type. Experts believe that people with antisocial personality disorder may be predisposed to commit violent crimes because they lack feelings for others and remorse for their actions. Today more attention is focused on BPD than any other personality disorder. Like antisocial personalities, people with BPD seem to have little control over their impulses, but their anger is more likely to be focused inward. Many borderline personalities engage in self-harm behaviors, and an estimated 1 in 10 commit suicide.

> Some people believe that personality disorders do not really exist—that the label is used for people who think or behave outside of the societal norm.

The main character in the 1999 movie *Girl, Interrupted* is based on the real-life experiences of Susanna Kaysen, who was diagnosed with BPD after being admitted to a psychiatric hospital for depression. Kaysen, just 18 years old at the time, already had a history of promiscuity and other risky behaviors. Worried about her self-harm and suicidal tendencies, doctors kept her in a psychiatric hospital for 18 months.

Cluster C: Fearful or Anxious Behaviors

For disorders in the final cluster, anxiety and fearfulness are a key personality trait. Cluster C includes avoidant personality disorder, characterized by social inhibition, hypersensitivity, and feelings of inadequacy; dependent personality disorder, characterized by an inability and/or unwillingness to take care of oneself or make decisions; and obsessive-compulsive personality disorder, characterized by preoccupation with orderliness and perfectionism.

One blogger describes the fears and motivations of avoidant personality types:

> We are a peculiar people; often others don't understand us. Our avoidant personalities cause others to wonder or to judge. But . . . we are particularly sensitive to what our environment contains. Hyper-vigilance and mistrust will often accompany our thoughts and though we may yearn in our souls for friendships, they often elude us. This leads to isolation for fear of rejection and a lack of acceptance amongst others.[9]

Avoidant personality disorder appears to affect as many people as BPD, but for most people the disorder is unrecognized and untreated—the result of their avoiding interpersonal relationships.

Are Personality Disorders Real?

Personality disorders are related to personality traits that all people have. For instance, while people with Cluster B personality disorders experience the same emotions that other people feel, their feelings are so intense that they have an overwhelming urge to act on them. People with some types of personality disorders have difficulty regulating their emotions and impulses.

The concept of personality disorders is controversial. Some people believe that personality disorders do not really exist—that the label is used for people who think or behave outside of the societal norm. In this

> **Unlike a physical disease that can be diagnosed through blood work or X-rays, diagnosis of a mental disorder relies heavily on subjective data derived from interviews and questionnaires.**

view, personality disorders are not in fact disorders but rather are extreme manifestations of a person's individual style. Others concede that there are some personality disorders, but that the diagnosis is applied too liberally. Even minor symptoms of disordered thoughts or odd behaviors, they say, can result in a diagnosis of a personality disorder.

On the other side are psychiatrists who believe that personality disorders are underdiagnosed—that many people have a disorder without knowing it. People who seek treatment for anxiety, depression, or other mood disorders are often found to have an underlying personality disorder. Experts caution that for each person who seeks help, there are probably many more who fail to recognize that they have a problem.

Difficulties in Diagnosis

One of the difficulties in determining the validity of personality disorders is the subjective nature of diagnosis. Unlike a physical disease that can be diagnosed through blood work or X-rays, diagnosis of a mental disorder relies heavily on subjective data derived from interviews and questionnaires.

Once a clinician has determined the presence of a personality disorder, he or she must determine which personality disorder is present. This is complicated by the co-occurrence, or comorbidity, of these disorders. Studies show that almost half of people with one personality disorder suffer from at least one other disorder at the same time. Some disorders appear to be more closely related than others. For instance, studies have found a disproportionate co-occurrence between paranoid personality disorder and schizoid, borderline, antisocial, and avoidant personality disorders. People with BPD appear to be particularly susceptible to developing another disorder or mental health problem. The more severe a disorder is, the more likely that a person will suffer from more than one personality disorder.

The criteria used to diagnose a personality disorder may be present in a variety of combinations. For instance, BPD has nine diagnostic criteria: desperate efforts to avoid real or imagined abandonment, unstable interpersonal relationships, identity disturbance, impulsivity, suicidal tendencies, mood swings, and chronic feelings of emptiness, intense anger, or paranoia. A diagnosis is found if a person has just five of these nine criteria. As a result, the disorder can look very different from one person to another. Another difficulty stems from the overlapping characteristics of personality disorders. Impulsivity is a criterion for several different disorders, while the inability to forge close relationships is a cornerstone of schizoid, schizotypal, and avoidant disorders.

Research shows that misdiagnosis is common. Misdiagnosis may be followed by months or even years of ineffective treatment and growing frustration among patients and their families. Tami Green writes of her struggle to get help for the

> " It is extremely difficult to diagnose personality disorders accurately in teens, as impulsivity and moodiness are part of 'normal' adolescence. "

symptoms of an undiagnosed BPD: "I went to therapist after therapist trying to find relief. In all of that searching, I never received a correct diagnosis for what was ailing me."[10] Like many others with a disorder, Green failed to recognize her symptoms and rejected the suggestion that her problems might be caused by mental illness. "Even with as much distress as I was in, I didn't believe I could have borderline personality disorder,"[11] she writes.

Personality Disorders in Children and Teens

Psychologists agree that personality is not fully developed until adulthood, so children are not usually diagnosed with personality disorder. Some character traits in children, however, can help to predict a personality disorder. Parents of adults with personality disorders often say that their children exhibited unusual behaviors from a very young age. Some parents of BPD patients, for instance, say their babies cried more than other babies, had more problems sleeping, were easily upset by changes in the routine, and were often difficult to soothe when upset.

Researchers have found components of avoidant personality disorder in infants as young as four months old, and most adults diagnosed with this personality disorder typically were extremely fearful and withdrawn toddlers. As children and teens, the avoidant personality has few friends and engages in few sports or other structured activities.

Adults with antisocial personality disorder often have a long history of getting in trouble throughout their school years due to difficulties both in controlling impulsive behaviors and in forging relationships with peers or adults. A 2008 study found that roughly 20 percent of adolescents diagnosed with oppositional defiant disorder or conduct disorder were later diagnosed with antisocial disorder, and 15 percent with BPD. Research also shows that ADHD is commonly a precursor of borderline and antisocial personality disorders.

Some psychologists suggest that early intervention may be the key to treating personality disorders successfully. Some go a step further to suggest that early diagnosis—in adolescence or even younger—is important. In the newest edition of the *DSM*, experts have added a provision for diagnosing BPD in adolescents. The *DSM* says that symptoms must be persistent for at least one year (compared with two years for adults). Experts caution that it is extremely difficult to diagnose personality disorders accurately in teens, as impulsivity and moodiness are part of "normal" adolescence. The symptoms of BPD also overlap with other mental health problems that may be present during teenage years, including depression, ADHD, and oppositional defiant disorder.

A New Approach

One of the defining characteristics of a personality disorder is that it is pervasive, but recent research has challenged this assumption. The notion of pervasiveness is particularly relevant to treatment, as it implies that the behavior is impossible to change. Some experts say that some mental health professionals may be hesitant to diagnose a patient with a personality disorder because the notion of pervasiveness suggests there is no cure.

In 2008 the American Psychiatric Association convened a work group of renowned psychiatrists to review the research and propose changes to the definition and diagnostic criteria for personality disorders. The work group has proposed a dimensional approach that would involve describing individuals along a continuum of behavioral traits, spanning normal and abnormal levels of functioning. The proposal would simplify the diagnosis by reducing the number of disorders from 10 to 5: antisocial/psychopathic, avoidant, borderline, obsessive-compulsive, and schizotypal types. Each type comes with a narrative paragraph description. The APA is currently conducting field trials to determine the effectiveness of the new approach.

What Are Personality Disorders?

66 **One of the hardest things about borderline personality disorder [is that] our emotions are so strong it can dictate our behavior, no matter how much you can intellectually understand your feelings as irrational. There is this overwhelming tension between my head and my heart, pushing and pulling me, as if I were wrestling an angel.** 99

—Amanda Wang, "Taking on the Challenge of Mental Illness," The Fight Within Us, February 16, 2010. http://blog.thefightwithinus.com.

Diagnosed with borderline personality disorder at the age of 27, Wang is making a documentary about her path to recovery.

66 **Extreme traits can be negative or 'dysfunctional' in the sense that they interfere with the achievement of socially or personally valued goals; however, they are not necessarily dysfunctions or disorders in the biological or medical sense.** 99

—Jerome C. Wakefield, "The Perils of Dimensionalization: Challenges in Distinguishing Negative Traits from Personality Disorders," *Psychiatric Clinics of North America*, September 2008.

Wakefield is a professor at New York University's Silver School of Social Work.

* Editor's Note: While the definition of a primary source can be narrowly or broadly defined, for the purposes of Compact Research, a primary source consists of: 1) results of original research presented by an organization or researcher; 2) eyewitness accounts of events, personal experience, or work experience; 3) first-person editorials offering pundits' opinions; 4) government officials presenting political plans and/or policies; 5) representatives of organizations presenting testimony or policy.

❝We need to establish a clearer boundary between normal and abnormal personality patterns.❞

—Joel Paris, "Recent Research in Personality Disorders," *Psychiatric Clinics of North America*, September 2008.

Paris is a research associate at the Sir Mortimer B. Davis Jewish General Hospital in Montreal, Quebec, Canada.

❝Personality disorders often begin in childhood and last through adulthood. There's some reluctance to diagnose personality disorders in a child, though, because the patterns of behavior and thinking could simply reflect adolescent experimentation or temporary developmental phases.❞

—Mayo Clinic staff, "Personality Disorders: Risk Factors," September 11, 2008. www.MayoClinic.com.

The Mayo Clinic is a leading medical practice and research nonprofit organization providing consumer information on health and medical issues.

❝Use of the borderline diagnosis clearly should be extended to adolescents; its clinical usage in this group is already extensive, its internal coherence and stability are established, and it predicts adult dysfunction as well as adult borderline personality disorder.❞

—John G. Gunderson, "Borderline Personality Disorder: Ontogeny of a Diagnosis," *American Journal of Psychiatry*, May 2009.

Gunderson is a professor of psychiatry at Harvard Medical School and director of psychosocial and personality research at McLean Hospital in Belmont, Massachusetts.

66 Because they are usually not overtly psychotic or blatantly manic, the person suffering from a personality disorder is, in some ways, far more frightening, insidious and dangerous to society. Outwardly, they look normal, function fairly well, seem socially-adjusted, and can be quite charming. But inwardly, they are deeply disturbed, wounded, manipulative, immature, self-centered, angry people. 99

—Stephen Diamond, "Masks of Sanity: Detecting Disguised Personality Disorders," Evil Deeds blog, *Psychology Today*, April 26, 2009. www.psychologytoday.com.

Diamond is a clinical and forensic psychologist in Los Angeles and the author of *Anger, Madness, and the Daimonic: The Psychological Genesis of Violence, Evil, and Creativity*.

66 Hollywood's iconic images of a vengeful Glenn Close in *Fatal Attraction*, a self-absorbed yet fragile Winona Ryder in *Girl, Interrupted*, or a masochistic Diane Keaton in *Looking for Mr. Goodbar* don't do a whole lot to help connect friends and family members to understanding loved ones who have been diagnosed with the disorder in a compassionate way. 99

—Amanda Smith, "Borderline Personality Disorder: Adventures in Recovery," Stop Walking on Eggshells blog, *Psychology Today*, May 19, 2010. www.psychologytoday.com.

After being diagnosed with borderline personality disorder, Smith founded the Florida Borderline Personality Disorder Association to help educate others about the disorder.

What Are Personality Disorders?

- Estimates for prevalence of personality disorders range greatly from one study to another; recent studies have shown rates ranging from **3.9 to 15.7 percent**.

- The 2009 World Health Organization's World Mental Health Survey estimated the prevalence for any personality disorder to be **6.1 percent**, which amounts to **3.6 percent** for Cluster A, **1.5 percent** for Cluster B, and **2.7 percent** for Cluster C (with some people having more than one disorder).

- Among young adults aged **19 to 25**, personality disorders are the second most common mental health problem, behind drug or alcohol abuse. The most prevalent disorders in the college students were alcohol use disorders (**20.37 percent**), followed by personality disorders (**17.68 percent**). In the noncollege students, personality disorders were most prevalent (**21.55 percent**), followed by nicotine dependence (**20.66 percent**).

- Roughly **30 percent** of patients in psychiatric hospitals have a personality disorder.

- The most common personality disorder appears to be **avoidant personality disorder**, which affects roughly 1 in every 20 Americans.

Types of Personality Disorders

Psychiatrists have identified specific personality disorders and put them into three categories. All of these disorders are pervasive patterns of thinking, feeling, and behaving that undermine a person's ability to function, but the symptoms and characteristics of the disorders vary widely.

Cluster A Personality Disorders	Paranoid personality disorder	• Distrust and suspicion of others • Believing that others are trying to harm you • Emotional detachment • Hostility
These are personality disorders characterized by odd, eccentric thinking or behavior and include:	Schizoid personality disorder	• Lack of interest in social relationships • Limited range of emotional expression • Inability to pick up normal social cues • Appearing dull or indifferent to others
	Schizotypal personality disorder	• Peculiar dress, thinking, beliefs or behavior • Perceptual alterations, such as those affecting touch
Cluster B Personality Disorders	Antisocial personality disorder	• Disregard for others • Persistant lying or stealing • Recurring difficulties with the law • Repeatedly violating the rights of others • Aggressive, often violent behavior • Disregard for the safety of self or others
These are personality disorders characterized by dramatic overly emotional thinking or behavior and include:	Borderline personality disorder	• Impulsive and risky behavior • Volatile relationships • Unstable mood • Suicidal behavior • Fear of being alone
	Histrionic personality disorder	• Constantly seeking attention • Excessively emotional • Extreme sensitivity to others' approval • Unstable mood • Excessive concern with physical appearance
	Narcissistic personality disorder Believing that you're better than others	• Fantasizing about power, success, and attractiveness • Exaggerating your achievements or talents • Expecting constant praise and admiration • Failing to recognize other people's emotions and feelings

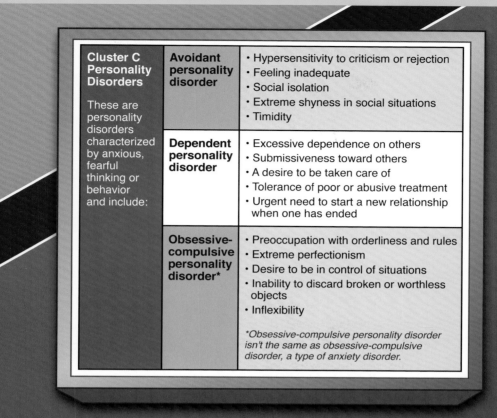

Cluster C Personality Disorders These are personality disorders characterized by anxious, fearful thinking or behavior and include:	Avoidant personality disorder	• Hypersensitivity to criticism or rejection • Feeling inadequate • Social isolation • Extreme shyness in social situations • Timidity
	Dependent personality disorder	• Excessive dependence on others • Submissiveness toward others • A desire to be taken care of • Tolerance of poor or abusive treatment • Urgent need to start a new relationship when one has ended
	Obsessive-compulsive personality disorder*	• Preoccupation with orderliness and rules • Extreme perfectionism • Desire to be in control of situations • Inability to discard broken or worthless objects • Inflexibility *Obsessive-compulsive personality disorder isn't the same as obsessive-compulsive disorder, a type of anxiety disorder.

Source: Mayo Clinic, "Personality Disorders: Symptoms," September 10, 2010. www.mayoclinic.com.

- Borderline personality disorder is the most common personality disorder among people in treatment: **30 to 60 percent** of patients with a personality disorder have borderline personality disorder.

- Borderline personality disorder is far more common than experts once thought. A 2008 study in the *Journal of Clinical Psychiatry* found that **5.9 percent** of Americans had borderline personality disorder, compared with 2000 estimates of 1 to 2 percent.

- The World Health Organization reports that personality disorders are significantly higher among people who **were unemployed, young, previously married, and poorly educated.**

Personality Disorders Among Young People

Personality disorders usually develop in late adolescence or early adulthood. According to a 2009 study, personality disorders are more common than mood or anxiety disorders in people between the ages of 18 and 24. The study also found that the overall prevalence of these disorders is lower among college students than their noncollege peers. In most cases, specific disorders are also less common in college students than their noncollege peers.

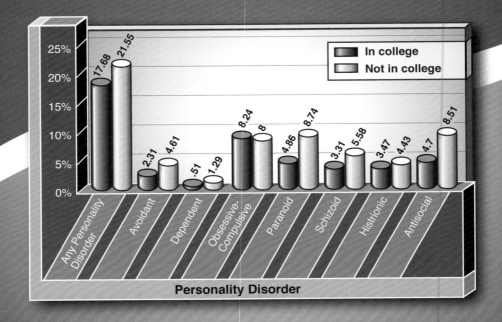

Source: Carlos Blanco et al., "Mental Health of College Students and Their Non-College Attending Peers: Results from the National Epidemiology Study on Alcohol and Related Conditions," *Archives of General Psychiatry*, December 2008. http://archpsyc.ama-assn.org.

- According to the National Institute of Mental Health, **45 percent** of those with any personality disorder meet criteria for two or more disorders.

- A 2010 study found that over **50 percent** of people with dependent personality disorder also had avoidant, obsessive-compulsive and/or borderline personality disorders.

Personality Disorders Linked to Other Mental Health Problems

Many people with personality disorders also have other mental health problems. This can make proper diagnosis difficult. More than two-thirds of people with a personality disorder also suffer from one or more Axis I disorders, which include anxiety disorders, depression and other mood disorders, attention deficit and other impulse control disorders, and substance abuse or dependence.

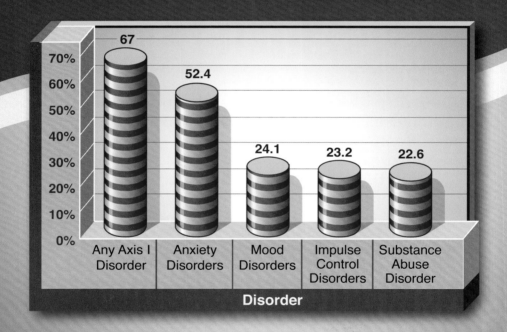

Source: Mark F. Lenzenweger et al., "DSM-IV Personality Disorders in the National Comorbidity Survey Replication," *Biological Psychiatry*, October 15, 2007. www.ncbi.nlm.nih.gov.

- Studies suggest that over **50 percent** of the people diagnosed with borderline personality disorder have another personality disorder at the same time; **25 percent** of BPD patients are diagnosed with antisocial personality disorder and **25 percent** with narcissistic personality disorder.

What Are the Causes of Personality Disorders?

> **"Personality disorders are thought to be caused by a combination of . . . genetic and environmental influences. Some research suggests that you may have a genetic vulnerability to developing a personality disorder and that your life situation may trigger the actual development of a personality disorder."**
>
> —Mayo Clinic, a leading medical practice and research nonprofit organization providing consumer information on health and medical issues.

> **"Borderline pathology is at least partially 'hard-wired,' involving brain abnormalities that can be identified by brain imaging techniques."**
>
> —John M. Oldham, chief of staff at the Menninger Clinic in Houston, Texas, and a professor of psychiatry at Baylor College of Medicine.

The exact cause of personality disorders is unknown, but both biology and home environment are thought to play a role. People may be born with some risk factors, while others may be triggered by physical or emotional trauma, stress, drug abuse, or physical illness. Psychologists do not fully understand the specific role that these factors play in any given disorder or individual.

The human brain serves as the "command center" of the human body, controlling everything we do and feel. Different parts of the brain serve different functions. The frontal lobe, at the front of the brain, for instance, controls a person's ability to reason and control emotions. The hypothalamus, a small structure at the base of the brain, automatically regulates body temperature, sleep, and appetite. The brain also controls emotions and mood.

Researchers believe that abnormalities in the structure of the brain may contribute to the risk of developing a personality disorder. People with brain injuries sometimes share the unusual emotions and behaviors of people with personality disorders. Studies using brain-imaging technologies, such as magnetic resonance imaging, have shown that the brains of mentally ill individuals often look different than those of their healthy counterparts. One study showed that people diagnosed with antisocial personality disorder had less gray matter (the part that contains nerve cells) in the prefrontal cortex than people without a disorder.

Other brain imaging studies have revealed that people with a personality disorder may have a smaller hippocampus, which regulates long-term memory, and/or amygdala, a small, almond-shaped structure deep inside the brain

> " Abnormalities in the structure of the brain may contribute to the risk of developing a personality disorder. "

that regulates emotions such as fear and aggression. Recent research also suggests that in people with a disorder, these parts of the brain may be more reactive to certain types of stimuli. For instance, in a study in which people looked at faces with various types of emotional expressions, people with borderline personality disorder (BPD) experienced stronger activation in their left amygdalas.

A 2008 study, which compared the brain function of BPD and non-BPD individuals playing a competitive game, showed greater activity in the non-BPD players' anterior insula, the part of the brain that is involved in emotional responses to all kinds of situations. Scientists speculate that this demonstrates why people with BPD (and other disorders) have problems with trust and understanding society's norms.

A 2009 study used magnetic resonance imaging to examine how the brains of people with BPD react to social and emotional stimuli, compared with those without BPD. The study showed that parts of the brain that were active in healthy people when responding to disturbing emotional scenes were inactive in those with BPD. "This research shows that BPD patients are not able to use those parts of the brain that healthy people use to help regulate their emotions," said Harold W. Koenigsberg, a professor of psychiatry at Mount Sinai School of Medicine, who headed the study. "This may explain why their emotional reactions are so extreme."[12]

The Role of Neurotransmitters

Neurotransmitters are chemical messengers that travel from one neuron to another at an amazing rate of speed—less than 1/5,000 of a second—allowing people to react instantly to pain or other stimuli. Scientists have identified roughly 50 different neurotransmitters, each of which is responsible for sending a different message to the billions of neurons in the brain.

Recent research into the function of these neurotransmitters has begun to yield some information about how they might influence emotions and behavior. Some forms of personality disorders occur when too many or too few neurotransmitters are present or when something interferes with the neurotransmitter's pathway. Serotonin, for instance, functions within structures of the brain that regulate emotions and reactions to stress. High levels of serotonin are associated with aggression and poor sleep quality. Low levels are associated with irritability, anxiety, lethargy, and suicidal thoughts and behaviors. Brain imaging studies have shown that people with various forms of personality disorders have higher or lower levels of serotonin.

Dopamine is another neurotransmitter that has been linked to personality disorders. Dopamine influences mood, experience of pleasure, and the regulation of body movement. Some studies have found that people with some types of personality disorder may

> " In interviews, people with personality disorders are more likely than healthy individuals to report a history of physical, sexual, or emotional abuse. "

have lower levels of dopamine than people without these disorders. Researchers speculate that lower levels of dopamine might explain why people with histrionic, borderline, or other personality disorders are unable to control impulses and emotions.

Research suggests that opioids—the chemicals that inhibit physical and emotional pain—may also play a role in some personality disorders. A 2009 study found that people with BPD had more receptors for opioids in the brain but lower levels of the chemicals themselves. Experts speculate that the self-harm tendencies of BPD patients may result from this imbalance: When pain is encountered, opioids fill the receptors. Other studies have shown that people with BPD have an increased capacity to read the facial expressions of people. Researchers believe that increased levels of oxytocin, a hormone stimulated by the pituitary gland, may contribute to their heightened reaction to other people's moods or emotions.

> " **The loss of a parent—whether through death, divorce, or abandonment—also increases the risk of a personality disorder.** "

Research into the chemistry of personality disorders is still in its infancy. The number of studies is on the rise, however, and scientists, mental health practitioners, patients, and their families hope that new findings will help provide insight into the causes and potential treatment of these disorders.

The Role of Genes

Scientists believe that personality—and therefore personality disorders—has a genetic basis. Studies consistently show a higher incidence of personality disorder among relatives: An adult child of a parent with BPD, for instance, is 10 or 12 times as likely to be diagnosed with a personality disorder than offspring of parents without the disorder.

One way that researchers assess a genetic component is by looking at twins. Researchers can compare similarities between identical twins, who share the same genes, and fraternal twins, who share only 50 percent of their genes. A genetic component is assumed when a disorder is found

having a problem. To hear them tell it they were merely the victims of the behavior of others. The pain of seeing our children in this condition was magnified by the professionals who didn't or couldn't help them yet never hesitated to blame us for the problem.[13]

Experts caution against jumping to conclusions about a patient's family relationships or childhood history. Blaming families adds to the stigma of a disorder by suggesting that it is someone's "fault." Some experts caution that placing blame on parents or childhood experiences can inadvertently encourage patients to continue to shirk responsibility for their actions. In some cases patients in treatment have turned against their families and blamed loved ones for causing their disorder. By undermining their support network, this increases the risk that treatment will be ineffective.

Nature and Nurture

While much of the research has focused on whether biological or environmental influences play a greater role in personality disorders, it appears to vary greatly from one person to another. Writing about BPD, Robert O. Friedel, a psychiatrist specializing in the disorder, explains:

> It is generally held that biological and environmental risk factors interact to reach a certain critical level of brain dysfunction in order for the symptoms of borderline personality disorder to become apparent. It appears that this critical degree of disturbance of brain function can be achieved by a large amount of biological risk that requires only a low amount of environmental risk, low biological risk coupled with high environmental risk, or intermediate levels of both.[14]

Current research is focusing on the interplay between genetics and the environment to learn more about the specific factors that are involved. Mental health professionals hope that the findings from such research will help professionals identify children at risk and engage in early intervention, as well as to advance treatment programs for adults with personality disorders.

What Are the Causes of Personality Disorders?

66 Of all environmental factors that place a person at risk for developing borderline disorder, those associated with poor or uninformed parenting appear to be the most important. 99

—Robert O. Friedel, "Causes," Borderline Personality Disorder Demystified, 2010. www.bpddemystified.com.

Friedel is a psychiatrist specializing in borderline personality disorder.

....

66 Evidence for an association between childhood maltreatment and adult psychosis is inconclusive. No clear link between personality disorder and maltreatment has been noted. 99

—Ruth Gilbert, Cathy Spatz Widom, Kevin Browne, David Fergusson, Elspeth Webb, and Staffan Janson, "Burden and Consequences of Child Maltreatment in High-Income Countries," Lancet, January 3, 2009. www.thelancetglobalhealthnetwork.com.

These experts from the United States, the United Kingdom, and Sweden teamed up to publish their report for the Lancet Global Health Network.

....

* Editor's Note: While the definition of a primary source can be narrowly or broadly defined, for the purposes of Compact Research, a primary source consists of: 1) results of original research presented by an organization or researcher; 2) eyewitness accounts of events, personal experience, or work experience; 3) first-person editorials offering pundits' opinions; 4) government officials presenting political plans and/or policies; 5) representatives of organizations presenting testimony or policy.

66 While we don't know how exactly Personality Disorders develop and what causes them, there is some indication that it is probably a combination of biological makeup and disposition in interaction with life experiences and the environment that are at the root of these difficulties. 99

—Simone Hoermann, "Early Attachment and Personality Disorders," Mental Help Net Blogs, July 8, 2010, http://www.mentalhelp.net.

Hoermann is a psychologist who specializes in psychotherapy for personality disorders, anxiety, and depression and a faculty member of Columbia University.

66 Having borderline personality disorder means we are impaired in a key area of brain function. This makes it especially hard for most people with borderline personality disorder to even understand that this is what we have. 99

—Tami Green, "My Story," Borderline Personality Support, 2008–2010. www.borderlinepersonalitysupport.com.

Green, who was diagnosed with BPD after trying to take her own life, is a life coach for others with the diagnosis.

66 Research indicates that individuals who have difficulty with impulse control and aggression have reduced levels of activity in their brains in a number of key locations. 99

—John G. Gunderson, "A BPD Brief: An Introduction to Borderline Personality Disorder," National Alliance on Mental Illness, 2006. www.nami.org.

Gunderson is a professor of psychiatry at Harvard Medical School and director of psychosocial and personality research at McLean Hospital in Belmont, Massachusetts.

66 In the vast majority of violent offenders with personality disorders, the role of biology and neurology . . . [have] been wildly overstated. 99

—Stephen Diamond, "Masks of Sanity: Detecting Disguised Personality Disorders," Evil Deeds blog, *Psychology Today*, April 26, 2009. www.psychologytoday.com.

Diamond is a clinical and forensic psychologist in Los Angeles and the author of *Anger, Madness, and the Daimonic: The Psychological Genesis of Violence, Evil, and Creativity.*

❝I think most of the people who are in mental hospitals have nothing wrong with them that's demonstrably biological. . . . Most of the people who are in mental hospitals are there for some sort of personal, social, economic reasons; many of them are there because they are peculiar, eccentric, they are poor, [or] nobody wants them.❞

—Thomas Szasz, "All in the Mind," radio broadcast, ABC Radio National, April 4, 2009. www.abc.net.au.

Szasz, a psychiatrist in private practice, has been an outspoken critic of traditional psychiatric practices and is the author of *The Myth of Mental Illness.*

....

❝Parenting behaviors, such as low parental affection or nurturing, [are] associated with an elevated risk of avoidant personality disorder when these children reached adulthood.❞

—David C. Rettew, "Avoidant Personality Disorder," Emedicine, March 4, 2008. http://emedicine.medscape.com.

Rettew is the director of the Pediatric Psychiatry Clinic at Fletcher Allen Health Care and an associate professor of psychiatry and pediatrics at the University of Vermont College of Medicine.

....

❝Examinations of adults with APD [avoidant personality disorder] indicate that childhood lack of involvement with peers and failure to engage in structured activities may persist through adolescence and adulthood. Conversely, adults who have had positive achievements and interpersonal relationships during childhood and adolescence were more likely to remit from APD as adults.❞

—David C Rettew, "Avoidant Personality Disorder," Emedicine, March 4, 2008. http://emedicine.medscape.com.

Rettew is the director of the Pediatric Psychiatry Clinic at Fletcher Allen Health Care and an associate professor of psychiatry and pediatrics at the University of Vermont College of Medicine.

....

Facts and Illustrations

What Are the Causes of Personality Disorders?

- Recent research suggests that over **50 percent** of the risk of developing borderline personality disorder is conveyed by genetic abnormalities. A 2008 study concluded that the degree to which borderline personality disorder is caused by inborn factors—called the level of heritability—is **68 percent** (roughly the same as bipolar disorder).

- **Genes** that increase risk for a personality disorder may be passed on by those people who have a personality disorder or a related disorder, such as bipolar disorder, depression, substance abuse disorders, and post-traumatic stress disorder.

- Roughly **half** of children of adults diagnosed with borderline personality disorder will develop the disorder themselves.

- Studies show that those with a **parent or sibling** with a personality disorder are **five times** more likely to develop borderline personality disorder.

- Rates of borderline personality disorder among **relatives** of adults with the disorder are **12 times higher** than among the general population.

- Children with **oppositional defiant disorder**—a pattern of disobedient, hostile, and defiant behavior toward authority figures—are four times more likely to be diagnosed with a personality disorder when they grow up.

Risk Factors for Antisocial Personality Disorder

Researchers believe that genetic and environmental factors contribute to personality disorders. One of the most widely studied personality disorders, antisocial personality disorder, is believed to be influenced by biology, psychology, and social and cultural factors. Researchers are particularly interested in determining the environmental and social factors that may contribute to this disorder so that early intervention can be implemented. Poor parenting and childhood traumas such as abuse are believed to be risk factors for antisocial personality disorder.

Biological Influences

- Genetic vulnerability combined with environmental influences
- Abnormally low cortical arousal
- High fear threshold

Antisocial Personality Disorder

Psychological Influences

- Difficulty learning to avoid punishment
- Indifferent to concerns of others

Social/Cultural Influences

- Criminality
- Stress/exposure to trauma
- Inconsistent parental discipline
- Socioeconomic disadvantage

Source: David H. Barlow and V. Mark Durand, *Abnormal Psychology*, Belmont, CA: Wadsworth Cengage Learning, 2009, p. 465.

Risk Factors for Schizotypal Personality Disorder

Like other personality disorders, schizotypal personality disorder is believed to be influenced by biology, psychology, and social and cultural factors. Researchers believe this personality disorder may share some genetic basis with schizophrenia. Social anxiety and isolation are core elements of schizotypal personality disorder.

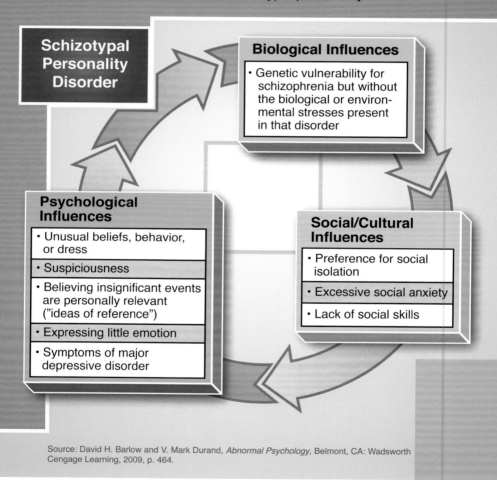

Schizotypal Personality Disorder

Biological Influences
- Genetic vulnerability for schizophrenia but without the biological or environmental stresses present in that disorder

Psychological Influences
- Unusual beliefs, behavior, or dress
- Suspiciousness
- Believing insignificant events are personally relevant ("ideas of reference")
- Expressing little emotion
- Symptoms of major depressive disorder

Social/Cultural Influences
- Preference for social isolation
- Excessive social anxiety
- Lack of social skills

Source: David H. Barlow and V. Mark Durand, *Abnormal Psychology*, Belmont, CA: Wadsworth Cengage Learning, 2009, p. 464.

- Young teenagers who show some signs of personality disorder are **25 times** as likely to have a personality disorder as adults.

- Twins studies have found a **35 percent** genetic effect for avoidant personality disorder; the majority (**83 percent**) of these genes are also related to other personality disorders.

- Studies show that **65 to 75 percent** of people diagnosed with BPD have been physically or sexually abused; **30 to 50 percent** lost or had a prolonged separation from their parents.

- **Sixty-one percent** of adults with avoidant personality disorder report childhood emotional abuse.

What Are the Effects of Personality Disorders?

❝[People] with personality disorder frequently behave in ways that others find baffling, odd, and come across as manipulative.❞

—Amanda Smith, founder of the Florida Borderline Personality Disorder Association, which works to help educate others about the disorder.

❝Borderline individuals are the psychological equivalent of third-degree-burn patients. They simply have, so to speak, no emotional skin. Even the slightest touch or movement can create immense suffering.❞

—Marsha M. Linehan, a leading expert on borderline personality disorder and the developer of dialectical behavior therapy.

Borderline personality disorder (BPD) has received much of the mental health profession's research in recent years, probably due to the high risk of self-harm behaviors and suicide. An estimated 10 percent of people with BPD commit suicide, and far greater numbers make one or more unsuccessful attempts. Three-quarters of people with BPD also engage in self-harm behaviors, such as cutting or burning themselves.

While other personality disorders have a much lower risk of suicide and self-harm behaviors than BPD, these disorders can be just as debilitating. The difficulties show up in different ways, depending on the nature of the disorder. People with avoidant personality disorder, for instance, may be so fearful of criticism that they refuse to leave home, or they might remove themselves from society to live far from human contact. People with obsessive-compulsive personality disorder may be unable to learn a new route to a familiar place or make the adaptations necessary to live with a new roommate or spouse.

The impulsivity common to several personality disorders also can lead to trouble. Some people with personality disorders are shopaholics, who cannot resist the urge to spend beyond their means. Indecisiveness and an inability to make decisions may hamper one's ability to get a job or rent an apartment. Some people with a personality disorder withdraw entirely from society, while others abandon themselves to a series of casual partners rather than risking intimacy with one person.

Trouble on the Job

Many people with personality disorders have difficulty finding a job or building a career. Anxious behaviors, such as obsessions and compulsions, may undermine a person's ability to accomplish even mundane, day-to-day tasks. Even among those who are able to hold down a job, a stressful event can cause a mental breakdown in which they cannot perform even routine mental tasks.

As in other areas of their lives, the problems encountered in the workplace may vary for different types of disorders. Difficulties with forming and maintaining relationships are often particularly problematic. People with narcissistic personality disorder, for instance, might get themselves in trouble by exaggerating their own accomplishments and demanding to be the center of attention, while those with avoidant personality disorder are more likely to be blamed for shirking work or failing to be part of a team. The eccentric behaviors and erratic emotions associated with personality disorders may impede a person's ability to interact with supervisors,

> " Even among those who are able to hold down a job, a stressful event can cause a mental breakdown in which they cannot perform even routine mental tasks. "

coworkers, and customers. People with some types of personality disorders may view a supervisor's commands as criticism or take a colleague's look or offhand comment the wrong way. One woman with BPD writes of her experiences trying to keep a job:

> I can't even count how many times I've been fired in the last 10 years. Failure I'm used to. . . . What's wrong with not being like everyone else? I can't do the lunch or break thing with people I work with. God, everything they talk about is soooooooooooooo boring! So I don't join in or I try to go outside and then everyone thinks I'm a snob. . . . I've come to the conclusion that Borderline Personality Disorder, rage and work just don't mix.[15]

When a Disorder Contributes to Success on the Job

Not all personality disorders are incompatible with workplace success; in fact, there is evidence that people with mild disorders can be highly successful. The heightened ability of those with BPD to read the emotions of others may be an asset in some types of work. Some say that the lack of a strong sense of identity typical of personality disorders can benefit an actor because it makes it easier to take on the personality of an assigned character. A 2005 British study found that senior executives in the business sector had significant elements of antisocial and narcissistic personality disorders. There is also anecdotal evidence that the charm exhibited by many narcissistic personalities can help them move up the organizational ladder. Still, success does not always translate to happiness. Sam Vaknin, author of *Malignant Self-Love: Narcissism Revisited* and an expert on narcissism, discusses the impact:

> Workplace narcissists seethe with anger and resentment. The gap between reality and their grandiose flights of fancy . . . is so great that they develop persecutory delusions, resentment and rage. They are also extremely and pathologically envious, seeking to destroy what they perceive to be the sources of their constant frustration: a popular co-worker, a successful boss, a qualified or skilled employee.[16]

Trouble at Home

Living with a personality disorder can be difficult not only for the person suffering from the disorder, but also for family, friends, and anyone else who is close—or attempts to be close—to this person. For many people with a disorder, even positive relationships are a source of stress. The fear of rejection and/or abandonment, low self-esteem, and inability to regulate emotions can result in emotional outbursts, verbal abuse, and sometimes even physical violence. This can strain relationships with even the most loving family members, who are often the sole emotional, moral, and financial support. "Being married to someone with BPD is heaven one minute, hell the next," says the spouse of a BPD patient. "My wife's moods change by the second. I'm walking on eggshells trying to please her and avoid a fight for speaking too soon, too quickly, in the wrong tone, or with the wrong facial motions."[17]

> "For many people with a disorder, even positive relationships are a source of stress. The fear of rejection and/or abandonment, low self-esteem, and inability to regulate emotions can result in emotional outbursts, verbal abuse, and sometimes even physical violence.

Tami Green, who was diagnosed with BPD at age 30, describes the impact on her life and that of her family:

> I lost my family, and I almost lost my life, to the ravages of this illness. I experienced all the common borderline disorder personality symptoms including feelings of emptiness, intense episodes of despair, anger to the point of rage, impulsivity, frantic attempts to avoid abandonment, pushing people who loved me far away, suicidal thoughts and behavior, and more. I often felt raw, exhausted, and pain that was too much to bear. My family and relationships suffered greatly, and I deeply wanted to die so the pain would stop.[18]

These problems are made worse by the fact that people with personality disorders often do not see themselves as troubled or recognize that they are suffering from a mental disorder. Many people with personality disorders blame their problems on others. They are convinced that their problems stem from the fact that relatives, friends, and/or colleagues mistreat or misunderstand them.

Parenting

People with personality disorders also may face difficulty as parents. They may be overemotional or extremely detached. One woman describes how her mother's personality disorder made her behave differently toward her family:

> She can be a very sweet person, especially to those outside our family, but if something doesn't go her way or she is in any way stressed, she snaps and is a different person. She is insanely controlling and was quite physically abusive to us as children. . . . When she had a "tantrum" and hit us, we were taken shopping and it was never mentioned again. She never apologized, just covered the pain with a gift. If I was to describe her behavior to an outsider, say someone who knows her from work, they would never believe my mother is capable of such terrible behaviors towards others.[19]

Unable to cope with the stress of parenting, people with a personality disorder may become emotionally, verbally, or physically abusive. This increases the risk that their children will later be diagnosed with a personality disorder.

Living on the Edge

The inability to function leads people with some personality disorders to live on the fringe of society. Many people with a disorder find it difficult to hold down jobs, and those that do often fail to be promoted to positions of authority. Their lower earning power contributes to the risk that these people will end up in marginal housing or homeless. Experts believe that many homeless Americans suffer from one or more personality disorders.

Some characteristics of particular disorders may add to the risk of marginalization. Schizoid or schizotypal personalities may find a home in the woods or live on the streets, where they will not have to deal with other people. People with paranoid personality disorder, for instance, may be attracted to cults that feed into their perception that the government or others are out to get them. Narcissistic personalities, on the other hand, may become cult leaders, with devoted followers who provide the adoration the narcissist craves.

Health Risks

Personality disorders appear to have a negative impact on one's mental and physical health. People with personality disorders are more likely than the general population to have recurring bouts of depression and anxiety. They also are at higher risk of an impulse control disorder, such as ADHD. Many people with personality disorders are more prone to obesity, eating disorders, and substance abuse—all of which increase the risk of a serious medical condition. Studies show that people with personality disorders are also more vulnerable to heart disease, diabetes, arthritis, and stroke.

Research shows that adults with BPD are considerably more likely to be victims of rape and other violent crimes, and that those with dependent personality disorders are at a higher risk of spousal abuse. Experts suggest that the vulnerability of people with a personality disorder may be due to their poor judgment in choosing partners and knowing whom to trust.

> " **Studies show that people with personality disorders are also more vulnerable to heart disease, diabetes, arthritis, and stroke.** "

Illnesses can be difficult to treat in a person with a disorder. Some forms of personality disorder are associated with hypochondria, a belief that real or imagined physical symptoms are signs of a serious illness. The continuing complaints and worries of a hypochondriac may blind family members to the symptoms of a real illness. In addition, people with a personality disorder often exhibit a paranoid distrust of others, including doctors. They may be unwilling to seek help for a medical problem, and when they do get help, they are less likely than others to follow the prescribed treatment regimen. Research shows that the presence of a personality disorder results in poorer outcomes for the treatment of other mental illnesses and physical diseases.

Criminal Behavior

Although the vast majority of people with personality disorders never commit a crime, a high percentage of criminals suffer from at least one personality disorder. The prevalence of antisocial personality disorder is far higher among incarcerated populations than the general public. Like people with other personality disorders, an antisocial person has difficulty controlling his or her impulses. In addition, the antisocial personality feels no guilt or remorse about breaking society's rules or hurting other people.

In *Abnormal Psychology*, David H. Barlow and V. Mark Durand point to Ted Bundy, a serial killer who preyed on dozens of women in the 1970s, as an extreme example of antisocial personality disorder. Bundy described himself as the "most cold-hearted son of a bitch you'll ever meet,"[20] who did not feel guilt for anything he did. Bundy did not hallucinate or become detached from reality; rather, his abnormal and erratic feelings and behaviors were part of his personality. Like Bundy, antisocial personalities may be intelligent and charming, which makes them even more dangerous to others.

Finding Success

Although many people with personality disorders have difficulty coping, the vast majority live and work among others unnoticed. Criminal behavior is rare, even among antisocial personalities. In fact, even people with severe forms of antisocial personality disorder can be highly successful if they channel their risk-taking impulses toward socially acceptable purposes.

Life can be challenging for anyone with a personality disorder. Those who succeed in coping and fitting into society often have strong support networks of family, friends, and professionals who help them recognize that they may not perceive the world as others do and help them change their behavior to meet society's norms.

What Are the Effects of Personality Disorders?

" [People] with personality disorders suffer a life that is not positive, proactive, or fulfilling. Not surprisingly, personality disorders are also associated with failures to reach potential. "

—Linda Labelle, "Personality Disorders," Focus Adolescent Services, 2008. www.focusas.com.

Labelle is the director of Focus Adolescent Services, an Internet site designed to help families with troubled and at-risk teens.

" I still REALLY struggle in almost every social situation I am in. I never feel like I actually 'fit in' with any group I am with. I find [it] extremely difficult to let down my guard and relax even with friends that I should feel at ease with. I live in a sort of self-imposed exile and the loneliness that causes is hard to handle. "

—Person with avoidant personality disorder, Avoidant Personality Disorder Forum, Psych Central, June 16, 2010. http://forums.psychcentral.com.

The forum for avoidant personality disorders is part of Psych Central, the Internet's largest and oldest independent mental health social network.

* Editor's Note: While the definition of a primary source can be narrowly or broadly defined, for the purposes of Compact Research, a primary source consists of: 1) results of original research presented by an organization or researcher; 2) eyewitness accounts of events, personal experience, or work experience; 3) first-person editorials offering pundits' opinions; 4) government officials presenting political plans and/or policies; 5) representatives of organizations presenting testimony or policy.

66 [BPD] patients have a rollercoaster life—they become intensely depressed or anxious very quickly; sometimes the intense mood swings can lead to suicide.99

—Harold Koenigsberg, Inside Mount Sinai, February 23–March 1, 2009. www.mountsinai.org.

Koenigsberg is a professor of psychiatry at Mount Sinai School of Medicine.

66 There are times, many times, that I can positively say how much I hate myself. I feel like I don't deserve to be alive. I feel like if I left today, no one would notice.99

—Amanda Wang, "Taking on the Challenge of Mental Illness," The Fight Within Us, February 16, 2010. http://blog.thefightwithinus.com.

Wang was diagnosed with borderline personality disorder at the age of 27.

66 I don't go into stores very much because I think that people are watching me through the security cameras and they will detain me for stealing something that I didn't steal. I also feel scared when I see a police car on the street because I am afraid that they will pull me over for something I didn't do.99

—"Poohbah," Paranoid Personality Disorder Forum, Psych Central, February 2, 2010. http://forums.psychcentral.com/showthread.php?t=134343&goto=nextoldest.

Poohbah suffers from paranoid personalitiy disorder.

66 A disorder that is often prompted by and occurs in the context of relationships, BPD can wreak havoc not only on those with the disorder but on their loved ones as well.99

—Perry D. Hoffman, "Borderline Personality Disorder: A Most Misunderstood Illness," NAMI Advocate, Winter 2007.

Hoffman is the president of the National Education Alliance for Borderline Personality Disorder.

66 **Living with a narcissist is a harrowing experience. It can tilt one's mind toward abnormal reactions (really normal reactions to an abnormal situation). . . . The narcissist has a way of getting under his partner's skin.** 99

—Sam Vaknin, "Narcissists, Paranoiacs and Psychotherapists," HealthyPlace, November 14, 2009. www.healthyplace.com.

Vaknin, a self-proclaimed narcissist, is the author of the book *Malignant Self-Love: Narcissism Revisited*.

66 **So why am I so worn out? I don't know what's coming out of his mouth yet, but I do know it isn't going to be anything good or happy. There is no happy for him.** 99

—"Twinkle," "Mixed State (Also Called Mixed Mania)," Experience Project, October 19, 2009. www.experienceproject.com.

"Twinkle" is married to a man struggling with the symptoms of borderline personality disorder.

66 **The true cost of personality disorder remains unknown, but it is certainly substantial, falling to many service providing sectors (health, social services, criminal justice) as well as to the economy more widely (inability to work and premature death).** 99

—Peter Tyrer, "Personality Disorder: A New Global Perspective," *World Psychiatry*, February 2010.

Tyrer represents the World Psychiatric Association Section on Personality Disorders.

What Are the Effects of Personality Disorders?

- A 2008 study of 18- to 24-year-olds found higher rates of personality disorders among **noncollege students** (21.6 percent) than college students (17.7 percent).

- In a study that examined the causes for **early discharge** from the military for psychiatric reasons, personality disorders accounted for **11 percent**.

- Major mental disorders cost the nation at least **$193 billion** annually in lost earnings alone, according to a 2008 study funded by the National Institute of Mental Health.

- In age-adjusted comparisons, almost **50 percent** of persons with schizoid personality disorder had fair or poor health, whereas only **11 percent** of persons without the disorder had fair or poor health; persons with schizoid personality disorder were at least twice as likely ever to have been diagnosed with heart or lung disease, diabetes, arthritis, or stroke than were persons without the disorder.

- According to the National Comorbidity Survey, **67 percent** of people with a personality disorder also have an Axis I disorder, such as depression or anxiety; only **24.8 percent** of people with an Axis I disorder also have a personality disorder.

Personality Disorders and Substance Abuse

Many people with personality disorders turn to drugs or alcohol, perhaps in an effort to help them deal with their extreme emotions. Almost one-quarter of people with a personality disorder are diagnosed with a substance abuse disorder as well. The high rate of substance abuse and dependence increased the risk that people with personality disorders will have health problems, and it interferes with treatment.

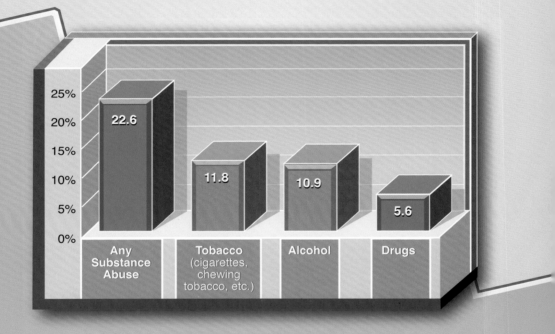

Source: Mark F. Lenzenweger et al., "DSM-IV Personality Disorders in the National Comorbidity Survey Replication," *Biological Psychiatry*, October 15, 2007. www.ncbi.nlm.nih.gov.

- An estimated **70 percent** of people with borderline personality disorder have dysthymia, a chronic form of mild depression, and **60 percent** will have at least one episode of major depression.

- Studies suggest that as many as **50 percent** of those with mental health issues develop addiction problems.

Personality Disorders and Spousal Abuse

Research shows that people with some types of personality disorder are more vulnerable to being victims of violence. In a 2009 study, researchers sought to explore whether people with dependent personality disorder were at greater risk of being abused by their spouse. The sample included 305 subjects receiving outpatient services for physical abuse. Researchers found that people with dependent personality disorder suffer spousal abuse far more often than people with other personality disorders or than people who do not have personality disorders.

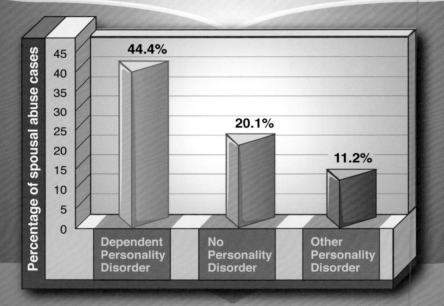

Source: National Library of Medicine, "Dependent Personality Disorder and Physical Abuse," May 26, 2010. www.nlm.nih.gov.

- An estimated **75 to 85 percent** of people with borderline personality disorder engage in **self-harm behaviors** such as cutting or burning. In one study, **96 percent** of women who had engaged in self-harm behaviors said they did so to get relief from their emotions.

- The odds of having 3 or more Axis I disorders are **10 times** greater in individuals with Cluster A personality disorders (paranoid, schizoid, and schizotypal) than in individuals without a personality disorder, **35 times** greater in individuals with Cluster C personality disorders (avoidant, dependent, and obsessive-compulsive) than in individuals without a personality disorder, and **49 times** greater in individuals with Cluster B personality disorders (antisocial, borderline, histrionic, and narcissistic) than in individuals without a personality disorder.

- In a 2008 study of patients who had been hospitalized for deliberate self-harm, **64 percent** of those aged 45 to 74 and **58.5 percent** of those aged 15 to 24 were found to have a personality disorder. In the younger group the most common type of personality disorder was borderline personality disorder (28.6 percent); in the elderly group, the most common type of personality disorder was obsessive-compulsive (36 percent).

- An estimated **65 to 75 percent** of people with borderline personality disorder attempt suicide; roughly **10 percent** succeed.

- The Institute of Medicine estimates that **90 percent** of persons who commit suicide suffer from a diagnosable psychiatric disorder at the time of their deaths; borderline personality disorder accounts for an estimated **35 percent** of the suicide rate.

- A study reviewing prison data from 12 countries found that **42 percent** of incarcerated women and **65 percent** of incarcerated men have at least 1 personality disorder. Prisoners are about 10 times more likely than the average population to have antisocial personality disorder.

Can People Overcome Personality Disorders?

❝The truth is, borderline personality disorder is highly treatable. I, and many others, are living proof of this.❞

—Tami Green, diagnosed with borderline personality disorder after trying to take her own life, is a life coach for others with the disorder.

❝A consistent finding from studies on the treatment of personality disorder is that, both in the short and longer term, those patients who present themselves for the treatment of their personality disorders show a steady improvement.❞

—Youl-Ri Kim, Department of Neuropsychiatry at Inje University College of Medicine in Seoul, Korea, and Peter Tyrer, Centre for Mental Health at Imperial College London and chair of the World Psychiatric Association Section on Personality Disorders.

Personality disorders are among the most difficult illnesses to treat. In fact, for many years, psychiatrists assumed that most disorders were untreatable. Borderline personality disorder (BPD), in particular, had a very poor prognosis. Psychiatrists Lois W. Choi-Kain and John G. Gunderson write, "In hospitals, BPD patients were referred to as 'help-rejecting complainers.' . . . At best, a diagnosis of BPD was a statement of therapeutic pessimism. At its worst, the diagnosis brought expectations of aggressive or hostile acting out against therapeutic efforts."[21]

Yet studies show that with effective treatment, even people with severe personality disorders can recover. The challenge is to get people into treatment, find the strategies that will work for the specific disorder and its symptoms, and provide the support people need during and following the treatment program.

Getting Help

For any type of personality disorder, treatment is generally more effective before behaviors are entrenched and symptoms are severe. Unfortunately, early treatment is rare. People with personality disorders often fail to recognize that a mental disorder is at the root of their difficulties. They tend to be unaware that their thoughts or behaviors are unusual and may be indifferent to the consequences of their behavior.

Many people seek help only after symptoms have caused a major disruption in their lives—perhaps after losing a job or important relationship. Some people seek help on the persistent advice of a loved one, while others may be forced into treatment after a criminal act or suicide attempt. Often, the help they seek is for anxiety, depression, or substance abuse, increasing the risk that the underlying disorder may go undiagnosed.

Some patients have a long history of hospitalization and institutionalization before being properly diagnosed. One mother writes of her attempt to get help for her daughter, who suffers from severe symptoms of a personality disorder:

> We spent years searching for the best facilities in the US and for the most suitable care for her. I visited nine hospitals and residential treatments centers. My daughter stayed in five of them. . . . Nothing worked. She was thrown out of every place except the last which she fled before they had a chance. Truckloads of meds were administered and hours of every kind of therapy under the sun was tried. The system failed her.[22]

Psychotherapy

Psychotherapy—or "talk therapy"—is the cornerstone of most treatment programs for personality disorders. Psychotherapy usually includes individual therapy sessions between a patient and psychiatrist or other mental health specialist. Therapy sessions are usually held at least once a week;

daily sessions might be used for patients undergoing a crisis. Because of the persistent nature of personality disorders, patients are typically in treatment for several years.

Cognitive behavioral therapy is effective for some personality disorders. The goal of cognitive behavioral therapy is to change a person's dysfunctional thought patterns and teach new skills for managing emotions and behaviors. Another common approach, called transference-based psychotherapy, focuses on changing the way people perceive themselves and others, and their environment. The main goal of these therapies is to help patients learn more effective ways of relating to people and reacting to situations.

Dialectical Behavioral Therapy

Dialectical behavioral therapy (DBT), which emerged in the 1970s to deal with hard-to-treat suicidal patients, may be effective in treating BPD and other severe forms of personality disorder. DBT combines aspects from several other treatment approaches. A key element is helping patients accept themselves as they are. Like cognitive behavioral therapy, DBT focuses on correcting distorted thought patterns and behaviors. Patients learn specific skills to control their emotions, rather than being controlled by them.

> **Because of the persistent nature of personality disorders, patients are typically in treatment for several years.**

Alexsandra Wixom, who at 25 has struggled with BPD for a decade, is among those who credit DBT with saving their lives. For 8 years, Wixom had met with psychiatrists biweekly, seeking help for extreme mood swings and emotions. She tried antidepressants, mood stabilizers, and antipsychotics. The drugs sometimes helped a little, but the effect was always fleeting. Wixom was in and out of psychiatric hospitals, seeking help in dealing with suicidal impulses. In 2007, after a prescription drug overdose, she was referred to Marsha M. Linehan, the psychiatrist who had developed DBT. Linehan diagnosed BPD and began a treatment program that included group and individual sessions. Within a year, Wixom was feeling better. "DBT is the best thing in the world. It saved my life," she says. "Nobody in my boat should be without this."[23]

Social Skills Training

Some patients with personality disorders need to learn basic skills, as well as ways of handling their own emotions. Michael Gray is a good example. Gray struggled for years with symptoms of avoidant and paranoid personality disorders. He did not like to go out, because he thought strangers were scrutinizing his every move and judging his behavior. He hated grocery shopping because he believed the checkout clerks judged his diet. He believed security guards followed him as he shopped. Prescription antianxiety medication helped a little, but he preferred to avoid going out altogether. Over time his avoidance techniques undermined his ability to take care of himself; at 36 he moved back in with his mother.

At the urging of his mother, Gray saw a therapist. Gray had not been shopping for many years, and his fear of new situations compounded his irrational fear of being criticized by others. Gray's therapist helped him recognize that his fears were unrealistic. She also mimicked the shopping experience in her therapy sessions, having Gray interact with her as she role-played the checkout clerk. After several sessions, the therapist took him shopping for real, applying the techniques they had practiced in therapy sessions.

> **Basic communication skills, such as learning how to start a conversation or read another person's body language, are often at the center of successful skill training.**

Such social skills training is often integral to successful treatment for personality disorders. Social skills training may help a person become more comfortable with activities of daily life or to tackle what they perceive to be an insurmountable goal, such as applying and interviewing for a job.

Basic communication skills, such as learning how to start a conversation or read another person's body language, are often at the center of successful therapy. Therapy also may be targeted to a specific anxiety, such as talking on the phone or entering a room full of strangers. Often, these skills are taught in group sessions.

In addition to enabling patients to practice the interpersonal skills, group therapy has the additional benefit of allowing patients to talk through issues and learn coping mechanisms from one another. Patients with some types of personality disorders may resist group therapy because it requires them to express their feelings or disclose personal information; some experts argue that a supportive group is essential to recovery for this very reason. Many patients with a personality disorder say that the support of others who are experiencing similar challenges has been instrumental in their recovery.

Drug Therapy

Some psychiatrists include prescription drugs as part of their treatment regimen for people with severe personality disorders. The most common classes of medications used for personality disorders are antidepressants, anticonvulsants and mood stabilizers, and antipsychotics.

Antidepressant drugs such as selective serotonin reuptake inhibitors (SSRIs) are often prescribed when a person complains of depression-like symptoms, including low self-esteem and thoughts of suicide. Antidepressants also may be effective in treating impulsivity. Anticonvulsant drugs are most commonly used for borderline or histrionic patients to help them balance their intense feelings and reduce impulsive outbursts and aggression. Low doses of a class of drugs called neuroleptics and antipsychotic medications such as risperidone or olanzapine are sometimes used to treat paranoia, mood swings, and/or disorganized thoughts.

> " **Drugs may help alleviate some of the symptoms of a personality disorder, but they will not affect the traits themselves.** "

These drugs can be helpful in stabilizing emotions, reducing impulsivity, and enhancing reasoning abilities in people with personality disorders, but the effectiveness of any drug is limited. Drugs may help alleviate some of the symptoms of a personality disorder, but they will not affect the traits themselves. For this reason, drugs are usually only prescribed to patients who are actively engaged in psychotherapy.

Factors Influencing Recovery

The road to recovery is often a long, involved process. "When I first started therapy I thought that if I just went to therapy and . . . answered the questions that they had asked me, I'd get better," says Amanda Wang. "The more we did that the more I got scared, the more I got frustrated . . . and angry because I didn't see any change in myself. I began to realize that therapy wasn't a passive relationship."[24]

Recovery depends on changing entrenched attitudes and behaviors, and people often feel worse before they feel better. Combined with the basic distrust that comes with many disorders, the difficulty involved in making such changes causes many patients to drop out of therapy. "My daughter is left with only her family to help her," writes Kristin Ulland, whose daughter suffers from severe symptoms of a personality disorder. "She doesn't trust doctors, psychiatrists or therapists."[25]

> **Recovery depends on changing entrenched attitudes and behaviors, and people often feel worse before they feel better.**

The effectiveness of treatment varies greatly according to the severity of the disorder and the specific symptoms. Studies of BPD patients show that severe forms of paranoid thinking tend to change most dramatically during remission, while other types of negative thinking about oneself ("I am not a good person" or "I am undeserving of love") may be more resistant to change. The research also shows that impulsive behaviors, including self-harm and suicidal tendencies, tend to change more readily than emotional symptoms such as depression, anxiety, anger, fear of abandonment, and the inability to tolerate being alone.

Some disorders appear to be more resistant to treatment than others. Studies show that Cluster A disorders may be more persistent than those in Clusters B or C. Research suggests that the elements of dependent personality disorder may be particularly resistant to change. Differences in outcomes may stem, at least in part, from the motivation of people suffering from the disorder. The greater the impact the disorder has on someone's ability to function, the more the patient might be willing to undergo the stress and unease of making a change.

Recovery and Relapse

People with a personality disorder may have to continue for many years to resist familiar patterns of thinking and behavior. Symptoms may recede, only to come back months or years later. Often a relapse is triggered by a stressful event. A new job or relationship can cause a person to relapse.

> **Today a number of promising treatment options are available, and tomorrow will bring still more, offering patients renewed hope for a better future.**

Patients who have experienced change offer hope to those who are struggling with a new diagnosis. "I have been through intense therapy, and it has gotten me farther in feeling better, thinking clearly, and being more secure with myself," writes one woman who has struggled with a personality disorder all her life. "After about 4 rocky relationships, [I] have found a wonderful, wonderful person who accepts me. [I still have to] work at getting better. . . . Although I know I am not fully cured I have gotten to a midway point and that shows that it must be possible."[26]

Into the Future

Within the psychiatric community and beyond, there is more attention to personality disorders than ever before. For instance, in 2010 the American Psychological Association began a quarterly journal devoted to the theory, research, and treatment of personality disorders. Advocacy groups such as the Treatment and Research Advancements Association for Personality Disorder and the National Education Alliance for Borderline Personality Disorder have been formed to increase awareness and encourage research about personality disorders. Mental health groups sponsor online forums where people suffering from personality disorders can ask questions of one another and get advice from mental health professionals. Many of these groups also offer referral services for people who believe they or a loved one has a personality disorder. Patients also have created Web sites to share information and blog about their journey to recovery.

The increased access to information offers new hope to those suffering from a personality disorder. In the past, many people were afraid to seek treatment for the troubling symptoms of a personality disorder because of the stigma that was sometimes attached to the disorder. Many people diagnosed with a personality disorder were given little hope: They had no choice but to live as best they could with the disorder and its debilitating symptoms. Today a number of promising treatment options are available, and tomorrow will bring still more, offering patients renewed hope for a better future.

Primary Source Quotes*

Can People Overcome Personality Disorders?

66 The diagnosis of borderline personality disorder conjures up thoughts of helplessness and hopelessness. The helplessness and hopelessness reside not only in the patient but often in the treatment providers as well. 99

—Kenneth R. Silk, "Augmenting Psychotherapy for Borderline Personality Disorder: The STEPPS Program," *American Journal of Psychiatry*, 2008. http://ajp.psychiatryonline.org.

Silk is a professor in the Department of Psychiatry and the director of the Personality Disorders Program at the University of Michigan.

66 BPD is a diagnosis with much more cause for hope than we once thought. Many people with BPD recover in only a few years, and, once they recover, their symptoms are unlikely to return. 99

—Alex Chapman and Kim Gratz, *The Borderline Personality Disorder Survival Guide*. Oakland, CA: New Harbinger, 2007.

Chapman is an assistant professor and registered psychologist in the Department of Psychology at Simon Fraser University; Gratz is a research assistant professor in the Department of Psychology at the University of Maryland and the director of the Personality Disorders Division of the Center for Addictions, Personality, and Emotion Research.

Bracketed quotes indicate conflicting positions.

* Editor's Note: While the definition of a primary source can be narrowly or broadly defined, for the purposes of Compact Research, a primary source consists of: 1) results of original research presented by an organization or researcher; 2) eyewitness accounts of events, personal experience, or work experience; 3) first-person editorials offering pundits' opinions; 4) government officials presenting political plans and/or policies; 5) representatives of organizations presenting testimony or policy.

(sidebar) Primary Source Quotes

❝I most definitely have [dependent personality disorder], but . . . I haven't been diagnosed [with] it because I refuse to go to my [doctor] alone, and without someone to hold my hand through it.❞

—"KellyWoo," "My Problem," Experience Project, July 30, 2009. www.experienceproject.com.

"KellyWoo" is a young adult who posted a message at Experience Project, an Internet social networking site.

❝Mental illness isn't an excuse to deny ourselves from being remarkable. Mental illness is the reason to be remarkable.❞

—Amanda Wang, "Taking on the Challenge of Mental Illness," The Fight Within Us, February 16, 2010. http://blog.thefightwithinus.com.

Wang was diagnosed with borderline personality disorder at the age of 27.

❝Unfortunately, structured treatments [for personality disorder] are not widely available. They can also be expensive. Since each clinician has his or her own unique 'brand' of therapy . . . finding the right therapist is a bit like searching for a job.❞

Paul T. Mason and Randi Kreger, *Stop Walking on Eggshells: Taking Your Life Back When Someone You Care About Has Borderline Personality Disorder*. Oakland, CA: New Harbinger, 2010.

Mason is vice president of clinical services at Wheaton Franciscan Healthcare in Racine, Wisconsin; Kreger founded and hosts www.bpdcentral.com, a Web site focused on helping and advocating for family members who have a loved one with BPD.

❝It is really a shame that there is not any medication to treat histrionic PD because this is a physical problem even though it manifests as mental symptoms. It affects one's entire life, and most people affected will not admit it and are certainly not organized or emotionally steady enough to agree to psychotherapy.❞

—Barbara, "Histrionic Personality Disorder: User Contributions," *Encyclopedia of Mental Disorders*, April 3, 2007. www.minddisorders.com.

Barbara, who is married to a man with histrionic personality disorder, believes her daughter has the disorder as well.

> **❝If 12-step recovery has taught me one thing, it's that to get better, you need to connect with someone who has gotten through it. To believe that you can survive, you need to see that someone else has done it.❞**

—Kiera Van Gelder, *The Buddha and the Borderline: My Recovery from Borderline Personality Disorder Through Dialectical Behavior Therapy, Buddhism, and Online Dating*. Oakland, CA: New Harbinger, 2010.

Van Gelder was diagnosed with borderline personality disorder when she was 30 years old.

> **❝Recent evidence . . . has shown that the supportive, involved family of a person with BPD has a measurable effect on the recovery of the individual. . . . We can be influential in our loved one's recovery and care for ourselves as well!❞**

—Diane Hall and Jim Hall, "Guest Post: Since Our Daughter's Diagnosis," The Fight Within Us, April 25, 2010. http://blog.thefightwithinus.com.

The Halls, whose daughter was diagnosed with borderline personality disorder in early adulthood, are family educators for the National Alliance on Mental Illness and the National Education Alliance for Borderline Personality Disorder.

> **❝I've spoken with more than a few parents and spouses who assume that their loved one would be trying 'harder' if they really wanted to recover.❞**

—Amanda Smith, "Borderline Personality Disorder: Adventures in Recovery," Stop Walking on Eggshells blog, *Psychology Today*, May 19, 2010. www.psychologytoday.com.

After being diagnosed with borderline personality disorder, Smith founded the Florida Borderline Personality Disorder Association to help educate others about the disorder.

> **❝While researchers have developed comprehensive psychosocial treatments for BPD, most patients improve with the help of treatment as usual as well as the support and guidance of those who care about them.❞**

—Mary C. Zanarini, "Reasons for Change in Borderline Personality Disorder (and Other Axis II Disorders)," *Psychiatric Clinics of North America*, September 2008. www.ncbi.nlm.nih.gov.

Zanarini is the director of the Laboratory for the Study of Adult Development at McLean Hospital in Belmont, Massachusetts, and an associate professor of psychology at Harvard Medical School.

66 My new goal is the truth. I avoid lying to myself or others—even small ones. It's hard but has become a habit like anything else you practice. I have found that being honest with myself has helped me to control some of the behaviors I'd prefer to avoid. I still have a way to go, but doesn't everyone? **99**

—HPDMIGHTBME, "Histrionic Personality Disorder: User Contributions," *Encyclopedia of Mental Disorders*, August 19, 2009. www.minddisorders.com.

HPDMIGHTBME is a blogger who has suffered from the symptoms of histrionic personality disorder for many years.

---

66 Personality disorders are among the most prevalent mental disorders, both in the community and in clinical practice. Psychodynamic psychotherapy is an essential element of their treatment. **99**

—Robert Michels, "Review, *Psychodynamic Psychotherapy for Personality Disorders*," American Psychiatric Publishing, 2010, www.appi.org.

Michels is the Walsh McDermott University Professor of Medicine and Psychiatry, Cornell University.

---

66 It is essential to increase awareness of borderline personality disorder among people suffering from this disorder, their families, mental health professionals, and the general public by promoting education, research, funding, early detection, and effective treatments. **99**

—U.S. House of Representatives, Resolution 1005, 2009.

The U.S. House of Representatives passed a resolution in 2009 making May Borderline Personality Disorder Awareness Month.

Facts and Illustrations

Can People Overcome Personality Disorders?

- Fewer than **1 in 3** adults with a personality disorder seek treatment.

- A 2008 study of young adults between the ages of 19 and 25 found that fewer than **25 percent** with mental problems receive treatment.

- Data indicate that an average of **5 years** elapse between the time a person reaches out to the medical community for help and the time when BPD is accurately diagnosed. A 2009 review of the treatment histories of patients with borderline personality disorder found that **34 percent** of patients were initially given the wrong diagnosis.

- The most common false-positive personality disorder diagnoses are bipolar disorder (**17 percent**), depression (**13 percent**), and anxiety disorders (**10 percent**).

- Personality disorder patients who do not have a substance abuse disorder are **four times** more likely to improve with treatment than those who abuse substances.

- A 2005 study shows that **88 percent** of patients with borderline personality disorder no longer meet the criteria for the disorder 10 years after starting treatment. Most show some improvement within a year.

- In a 2006 study comparing patients on dialectical behavioral therapy and other techniques, suicidal patients engaged in the therapy had **half the rate** of **attempted suicides** over the next two years and were hospitalized less often for **suicidal thoughts**.

Personality Disorder Hospitalizations in the United Kingdom

With treatment, often including hospitalization, people can overcome personality disorders. According to data collected by the UK Department of Health, almost two-thirds of personality disorder patients admitted to hospitals in the United Kingdom between 2006 and 2007 were admitted for borderline personality disorder (listed as "emotionally unstable," the term used by the World Health Organization).

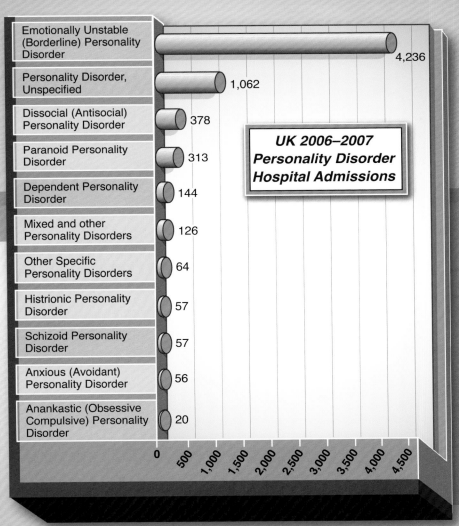

UK 2006–2007 Personality Disorder Hospital Admissions

Emotionally Unstable (Borderline) Personality Disorder	4,236
Personality Disorder, Unspecified	1,062
Dissocial (Antisocial) Personality Disorder	378
Paranoid Personality Disorder	313
Dependent Personality Disorder	144
Mixed and other Personality Disorders	126
Other Specific Personality Disorders	64
Histrionic Personality Disorder	57
Schizoid Personality Disorder	57
Anxious (Avoidant) Personality Disorder	56
Anankastic (Obsessive Compulsive) Personality Disorder	20

Source: UK Department of Health, "Hospital Episode Statistics," 2008.

Hospitalizations for Personality Disorders by Gender

Personality disorders appear to affect men and women differently. As can be seen from this chart, which compares the percentage of men and women who were diagnosed with a personality disorder after being admitted to a hospital, women tend to seek treatment more than men do. The chart also suggests that men are diagnosed more often with anti-social, schizoid, or obsessive-compulsive personality disorder, while more women suffer from borderline or histrionic personality disorder.

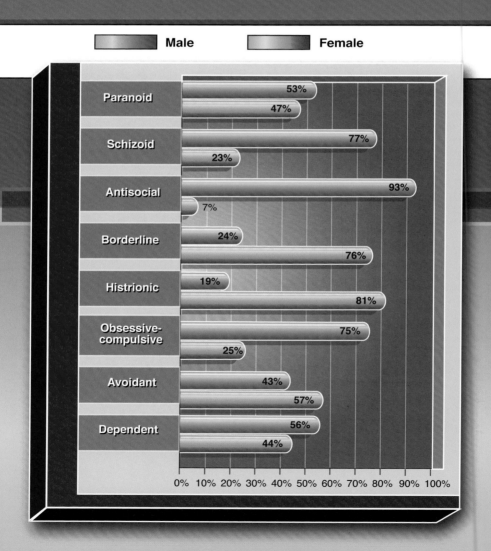

Source: UK Department of Health, "Hospital Episode Statistics," 2008.

BPD Treatment Programs Work

Professionals once believed that people diagnosed with BPD would not recover, but recent studies have shown that people who receive appropriate treatment can—and do—recover from the disorder. Patients are considered to have BPD if they have 5 of the 9 criteria outlined in the *Diagnostic and Statistical Manual*. In the study shown here, researchers recorded how many of these criteria patients met at the beginning of treatment and how many they had every 2 years after starting treatment. As can be seen from the graph, within just 2 years of beginning treatment, most BPD patients suffered from fewer symptoms of the disorder. Perhaps even more encouraging, the symptoms continued to abate over the next 10 years.

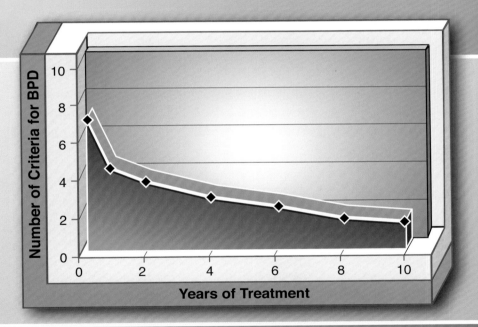

Source: John G. Gunderson, "Borderline Personality Disorder: Ontogeny of a Diagnosis," *American Journal of Psychiatry*, May 2009, p. 535.

- Patients with borderline personality disorder often need extensive mental health services and account for more than **20 percent of psychiatric hospitalizations.**

Key People and Advocacy Groups

Robert O. Friedel: Friedel, currently a professor of psychiatry at Virginia Commonwealth University, is an expert on borderline personality disorder. Friedel has written several books on the topic, including *Borderline Personality Disorder Demystified*, and hosts the related Web site Borderline Personality Disorders Demystified.

Tami Green: Green suffered intense feelings of emptiness, despair, and rage before she was diagnosed with borderline personality disorder as an adult. She now shares her story in an attempt to inspire others suffering from the disorder to seek treatment and serves as a life coach for people with borderline personality disorder and their family members, friends, and coworkers.

John G. Gunderson: Gunderson, a professor at Harvard Medical School and the director of psychosocial and personality research at McLean Hospital in Belmont, Massachusetts, is a leading researcher in the causes of and treatment for personality disorders.

Perry D. Hoffman: Hoffman is on the faculty of the Mount Sinai School of Medicine and is the president of the National Education Alliance for Borderline Personality Disorder, a nonprofit organization that works to raise public awareness, provide education, and promote research about the disorder. She has helped design programs for families of people with borderline personality disorder.

Susanna Kaysen: After being admitted to a psychiatric hospital in the 1960s, Kaysen was diagnosed with borderline personality disorder. Her 1993 memoir of her experiences during her 18-month hospitalization became the basis for the movie *Girl, Interrupted*.

Marsha M. Linehan: Linehan developed dialectical behavior therapy to treat the specific symptoms of borderline personality disorder. In addition to continuing research into the effectiveness of this therapy and other approaches, Linehan founded Behavioral Tech to train providers in these approaches.

National Alliance on Mental Illness (NAMI): The NAMI is a grassroots organization that advocates on behalf of the mentally ill through awareness campaigns, educational programs, and research. The NAMI included borderline personality disorder as a research focus in 2007.

Valerie Porr: After her daughter developed borderline personality disorder, Porr became an outspoken advocate for borderline personality disorder patients and families. In 1994 she founded the Treatment and Research Advancements National Association for Personality Disorder to reduce the stigma of the disorder and remains the organization's executive director.

Thomas Szasz: Szasz is an outspoken critic of the moral and scientific foundations of psychiatry and the function of psychotherapy. In his landmark book, *The Myth of Mental Illness*, published in 1960, Szasz argues that there is no such thing as mental illness or psychotherapy.

Amanda Wang: Since being diagnosed with borderline personality disorder in 2007, Wang has shared her experiences struggling with the disorder and the road to recovery. She hosts a Web site where she shares her story and interviews experts.

Mary C. Zanarini: Zanarini, the director of the Laboratory for the Study of Adult Development at McLean Hospital in Belmont, Massachusetts, and associate professor of psychology at Harvard Medical School, is a leading researcher in the effectiveness of treatment for borderline personality disorder.

Chronology

1952
The American Psychiatric Association publishes the *Diagnostic and Statistical Manual of Mental Disorders (DSM)*, marking the first comprehensive approach to classifying mental illnesses and defining diagnostic criteria.

1848
Phineas P. Gage survives an explosion in which an iron rod is driven into his brain, but his personality is drastically altered, providing the first clear evidence of the link between brain function and personality.

1938
American psychiatrist Adolph Stern chronicles a new type of disorder, on the "border" between neuroses and psychoses—a classification that grew into the category today known as personality disorders.

1886
Sigmund Freud begins providing therapy to mentally distressed patients in Vienna, Austria. Over the next couple of decades, Freud introduces psychoanalysis and theories that people are motivated by powerful unconscious drives.

1850   **1900**   **1940**

1954
Research undertaken by neuroscientist Wilder G. Penfield shows the first evidence of the relationship between chemical activity in the brain and psychological disturbance, ushering in an era of research on the role that biology plays in personality.

1879
Wilhelm Wundt founds the first psychology laboratory at the University of Leipzig, dedicated to the study of human emotions, behaviors, and cognitions.

1942
The Minnesota Multiphasic Personality Inventory is developed; it is still used to help identify personality traits and disorders.

1906
The *Journal of Abnormal Psychology* becomes the first journal sharing research and information about mental illnesses.

1949
The National Institute of Mental Health is created to carry out psychiatric education and research called for in the 1948 National Mental Health Act.

1950
In *Childhood and Society,* psychotherapist and researcher Erik Erikson expands on Freud's theories of personality to include social aspects of personality development at all ages of life; later experts theorize that disorders occur when social aspects do not develop appropriately.

1967
Psychoanalyst Otto Kernberg is the first to use the term *borderline* to describe patients whose symptoms are between psychoses and neuroses; the term is still used for one of the most common and difficult-to-treat personality disorders.

1976
The first tool to assess personality disorders is developed. The Personality Assessment Schedule identifies 24 dimensions of personality characteristics commonly found in personality disorders.

1980
The American Psychiatric Association includes diagnostic criteria for personality disorders in the third edition of its *Diagnostic and Statistical Manual.* Ten personality disorders are divided into three clusters.

2010
A brain imaging study confirms research suggesting that people with borderline personality disorder process pain stimuli differently than people without personality disorders, giving new insights into the reasons behind cutting and other self-harm behaviors common among BPD patients.

1965   **1980** **2005**   **2010**

1970s
Psychology professor Marsha M. Linehan introduces dialectical behavior therapy to help chronically suicidal clients. Over the next few decades, this therapy becomes a key treatment for borderline personality disorder.

2007
The National Alliance on Mental Illness adds borderline personality disorder as a research focus.

2008
The American Psychiatric Association's *DSM-V* Personality Disorders Work Group proposes changing the way personality disorders are diagnosed and recommends condensing them so that there are 5 rather than 10 types.

1977
Alexander Thomas publishes *Temperament and Development,* a landmark study exploring the relationship between temperament, the development of personality, and behavioral problems.

2009
The U.S. House of Representatives declares May as Borderline Personality Disorder Month, bringing new attention to this disorder.

Related Organizations

American Psychiatric Association

1000 Wilson Blvd., Suite 1825

Arlington, VA 22209

phone: (703) 907-7300

e-mail: apa@psych.org • Web site: www.psych.org

The American Psychiatric Association is a membership organization with more than 38,000 psychiatrists and other physicians working to ensure effective diagnosis and treatment for people with mental disorders. The association engages in a wide range of research and education activities and publishes the *American Journal of Psychiatry*.

American Psychological Association

750 First St. NE

Washington, DC 20002

phone: (800) 374-2721

Web site: www.apa.org

With 150,000 members, the American Psychological Association is the largest association of psychologists worldwide. Its mission is to advance the creation, communication, and application of psychological knowledge to benefit society and improve people's lives.

Behavioral Tech

4556 University Way NE, Suite 200

Seattle, WA 98105

phone: (206) 675-8588

e-mail: information@behavioraltech.org

Web site: www.behavioraltech.com

Behavioral Tech is a clearinghouse of information on dialectical behavioral therapy, providing referral, training, and resources for professionals, patients, and families of borderline personality disorder and other patients.

Mental Health America

2000 N. Beauregard St.

Alexandria, VA 22311

phone: (800) 969-6642

Web site: www.nmha.org

Mental Health America (formerly known as the National Mental Health Association) seeks to promote mental wellness by educating the public; fighting for access to effective care; fostering innovation in research, practice, services, and policy; and providing support to individuals and families living with mental illness and substance use problems.

National Alliance on Mental Illness (NAMI)

2107 Wilson Blvd.

Arlington, VA 22201-3042

phone: (703) 524-7600

Web site: www.nami.org.

The NAMI is a grassroots mental health advocacy organization. Since it began in 1979, the NAMI has engaged in a wide range of support, awareness, education, advocacy, and research programs to improve the lives of individuals and families affected by mental illness.

National Institute of Mental Health (NIMH)

6001 Executive Blvd.

Bethesda, MD 20892-9663

phone: (301) 443-4513; toll free: (866) 615-6464

Web site: www.nimh.nih.gov

The mission of the NIMH, which is part of the National Institutes of Health, is to transform the understanding and treatment of mental illnesses through research, paving the way for prevention, recovery, and cure. The organization offers information about diagnosis, causes, and treatment of personality disorders.

National Mental Health Consumers' Self-Help Clearinghouse

1211 Chestnut St., Suite 1207

Philadelphia, PA 19107

phone: (215) 751-1810 • fax: (215) 636-6312

e-mail: info@mhselfhelp.org • Web site: www.mhselfhelp.org

The National Mental Health Consumers' Self-Help Clearinghouse provides assistance for those suffering from a mental illness. The Clearinghouse works to foster consumer empowerment through its Web site, which offers news and information, a directory of consumer-driven services, publications, training packages, and individual and on-site consultation.

For Further Research

Books

Blaise A. Aguirre, *Borderline Personality Disorder in Adolescents*. Beverley, MA: Fair Winds, 2007.

Carol W. Berman, *Personality Disorders: A Practical Guide*. Philadelphia: Lippincott Williams & Wilkins, 2009.

Alex Chapman and Kim Gratz, *The Borderline Personality Disorder Survival Guide*. Oakland, CA: New Harbinger, 2007.

Duane L. Dobbert, *Understanding Personality Disorders: An Introduction*. Westport, CT: Praeger, 2007.

Martin Kantor, *The Essential Guide to Overcoming Avoidant Personality Disorder*. Santa Barbara, CA: ABC-CLIO, 2010.

Paul T. Mason and Randi Kreger, *Stop Walking on Eggshells: Taking Your Life Back When Someone You Care About Has Borderline Personality Disorder*. Oakland, CA: New Harbinger, 2010.

John M. Oldham, Andrew E. Skodol, and Donna S. Bender, eds., *Essentials of Personality Disorders*. Arlington, VA: American Psychiatric Publishing, 2009.

Jeffrey C. Wood, *The Cognitive Behavioral Therapy Workbook for Personality Disorders*. Oakland, CA: New Harbinger, 2010.

Periodicals

John Cloud, "The Mystery of Borderline Personality Disorder," *Time*, January 8, 2009.

Robert Langreth and Rebecca Ruiz, "The Forgotten Patients," *Forbes*, September 13, 2010.

Web Sites

Borderline Personality Disorder Demystified (www.bpddemystified.com). Written by Robert O. Friedel, a psychiatrist who specializes in borderline personality disorder, this Web site includes a wealth of information about borderline personality disorder diagnosis, treatment, and resources.

Borderline Personality Disorder, Facing the Facts (www.bpdfamily. com). This site designed for family members of people with borderline personality disorder includes a message board, articles, and links to support groups and books.

The Borderline Sanctuary (www.mhsanctuary.com/borderline). This Web site provides borderline personality disorder education, communities, support, books, and resources.

BPD Central (www.bpdcentral.com). Geared primarily toward family members and loved ones of people with borderline personality disorder, this Web site provides a wealth of information about causes, symptoms, and treatment options, as well as links to other related sites.

Personality Disorders, Mental Help Net (www.mentalhelp.net/poc/ center_index.php?cn=8). This Web site, hosted by the U.S. National Library of Medicine and the National Institutes of Health, includes articles written by professionals describing personality disorders and their symptoms, and links to related Internet resources.

Personality Disorders, Merck Online Medical Library (www.merck. com/mmhe/sec07/ch105/ch105a.html#sec07-ch105-ch105a-425). Based on the world's most widely used textbook of medicine—*The Merck Manual*—but written in everyday language, this Web site explains disorders, who is likely to get them, their symptoms, how they are diagnosed, and options available for prevention and treatment.

Treatment and Research Advancements National Association for Personality Disorder (www.tara4bpd.org). This Web site includes educational materials on borderline personality disorder, information on support groups for people with the disorder and their families, and a nationwide referral program that identifies clinicians and treatment programs designed for personality disorders.

Source Notes

Overview

1. Amanda Wang, "BPD Profile: Struggles, Breakdown & Breakthrough," RethinkBPD, YouTube video, September 26, 2009. www.youtube.com.
2. Amanda Wang, "Taking on the Challenge of Mental Illness," The Fight Within Us, February 16, 2010. http://blog.thefightwithinus.com.
3. *Diagnostic and Statistical Manual of Mental Disorders: DSM-IV-TR*. Washington, DC: American Psychiatric Association, 2000, p. 689.
4. Quoted in Lois W. Choi-Kain and John G. Gunderson, "Borderline Personality Disorder and Resistance to Treatment," *Psychiatric Times*, July 30, 2009. www.psychiatrictimes.com.
5. PsychologyNet, "Dependent Personality Disorder." www.psychologynet.org.
6. Quoted in Paul T. Mason and Randi Kreger, *Stop Walking on Eggshells: Taking Your Life Back When Someone You Care About Has Borderline Personality Disorder*. Oakland, CA: New Harbinger, 2010, p. 12.
7. A.J. Mahari, "Borderline Personality Disorder Inside Out," Borderline Personality. http://borderlinepersonality.ca.

What Are Personality Disorders?

8. Stephen Diamond, "Terrorism, Resentment, and the Unabomber," *Psychology Today*, April 8, 2008. www.psychologytoday.com.
9. Quoted in Avoidant Personality Disorder, 2010. www.avoidantpersonality.com.
10. Tami Green, "My Story," Borderline Personality Support, 2008–2010. www.borderlinepersonalitysupport.com.
11. Green, "My Story."

What Are the Causes of Personality Disorders?

12. Quoted in Mount Sinai School of Medicine, "Mount Sinai Research Identifies Brain Mechanisms Associated with Borderline Personality Disorder," press release, Mount Sinai School of Medicine, September 3, 2009. www.mssm.edu.
13. Valerie Porr, "From Grief to Advocacy: A Mother's Odyssey," Kathi's Mental Health Review, ToddlerTime Network. www.toddlertime.com.
14. Robert O. Friedel, "Causes," Borderline Personality Disorder Demystified, 2010. www.bpddemystified.com.

What Are the Effects of Personality Disorders?

15. Breaking Free, "Borderline Personality Disorder, Rage, and Work Don't Mix," The Borderline Experience: BPD Up Close and Personal, May 19, 2010. http://theborderlineexperience.com.
16. Quoted in HealthyPlace, "Narcissism in the Workplace," April 18, 2007. www.healthyplace.com.
17. Quoted in Mason and Krieger, *Stop Walking on Eggshells*, p. 11.
18. Green, "My Story."
19. Quoted in CounsellingResource.com, "Dealing with a Mother with a Personality Disorder," February 19, 2008. http://counsellingresource.com.

20. Quoted in David H. Barlow and V. Mark Durand, *Abnormal Psychology*, 4th ed. Belmont, CA: Wadsworth, 2004, p. 408.

Can People Overcome Personality Disorders?

21. Choi-Kain and Gunderson, "Borderline Personality Disorder and Resistance to Treatment."
22. Kirsten Ulland, "Guest Post: Between Mother and Child," The Fight Within Us, June 4, 2010, http://blog.thefight withinus.com.
23. Quoted in Robert Langreth and Rebecca Ruiz, "The Forgotten Patients," *Forbes*, September 13, 2010, p. 32.
24. Amanda Wang, "Frank Yeomans: BPD, Treatment & Assumptions," Rethink BPD, 2010. http://vimeo.com/10128863.
25. Ulland, "Guest Post."
26. "TwilightStar," "Borderline Personality Disorder Community," MedHelp, March 20, 2010. www.medhelp.org.

List of Illustrations

Index

Note: Page numbers in boldface indicate illustrations.

About the Author

Lydia Bjornlund is a writer in northern Virginia, where she lives with her husband, Gerry Hoetmer, and their twins, Jake and Sophia. She has written dozens of books for teens and young adults, specializing in issues related to American history and health. She holds a master's degree in education from Harvard University and a bachelor of arts from Williams College.